# MARTYRDOM

## CHRISTIANS IN THE ROMAN EMPIRE

**PUBLIC PERSECUTIONS**     Andrew Coddington

Cavendish
Square
New York

Published in 2017 by Cavendish Square Publishing, LLC
243 5th Avenue, Suite 136, New York, NY 10016

Copyright © 2017 by Cavendish Square Publishing, LLC
First Edition

Website: cavendishsq.com

This publication represents the opinions and views of the author based on his or her personal experience, knowledge, and research. The information in this book serves as a general guide only. The author and publisher have used their best efforts in preparing this book and disclaim liability rising directly or indirectly from the use and application of this book.

CPSIA Compliance Information: Batch #CW17CSQ

All websites were available and accurate when this book was sent to press.

Library of Congress Cataloging-in-Publication Data

Names: Coddington, Andrew, author.
Title: Martyrdom : Christians in the Roman empire / Andrew Coddington.
Description: New York : Cavendish Square Publishing, [2017] | Series: Public persecutions | Includes bibliographical references and index.
Identifiers: LCCN 2016033891 (print) | LCCN 2016035813 (ebook) | ISBN 9781502623270 (library bound) | ISBN 9781502623287 (E-book)
Subjects: LCSH: Christian martyrs–Rome–History–Juvenile literature.
Classification: LCC BR1604.23 .C63 2017 (print) | LCC BR1604.23 (ebook) | DDC 272/.1–dc23
LC record available at https://lccn.loc.gov/2016033891

Editorial Director: David McNamara
Editor: Fletcher Doyle
Copy Editor: Nathan Heidelberger
Associate Art Director: Amy Greenan
Designer: Jessica Nevins
Production Coordinator: Karol Szymczuk
Photo Research: J8 Media

The photographs in this book are used by permission and through the courtesy of: Cover Fine Art Images/Heritage Images/Getty Images; p. 4 MOIRENC Camille/hemis.fr/Getty Images; p. 7 Daniel Case/File:Statue on pedestal in courtyard at Church of the Nativity, Bethlehem.jpg/Wikimedia Commons; p. 8 Radius Images/Alamy Stock Photo; p. 11 George Adam Smith/File:Western Asia 4th-2nd centuries Smith 1915.jpg/Wikimedia Commons; p. 15 Universal History Archive/Getty Images; p. 17 Renata Sedmakova/Shutterstock.com; p. 23 Orazio Samacchini/ Rocca Sanvitale, Sala Baganza, Parma, Italy/Ghigo Roli/Bridgeman Images; p. 25 Culture Club/Hulton Archive/ Getty Images; p. 31 Renata Sedmakova/Shutterstock.com; p. 32 CosminConstantin Sava/Alamy Stock Photo; p. 34 Lebrecht Music and Arts Photo Library/Alamy Stock Photo; p. 37 jorisvo/Shutterstock.com; p. 43 Fine Art Images/Heritage Images/Getty Images; p. 50 Francis G. Mayer/Corbis/VCG/Getty Images; p. 58 Public Domain/File:Crucifixión de San Pedro por Francisco Ribalda.jpeg/Wikimedia Commons; p. 63 Fototeca Gilardi/ Hulton Archive/Getty Images; p. 67 Public Domain/File:Siemiradski Fackeln.jpg/Wikimedia Commons; p. 70 Mary Evans Picture Library Ltd/AGE Fotostock; p. 76 De Agostini/G. Cargagna/Getty Images; p. 85 Antiqua Print Gallery/Alamy Stock Photo; p. 88 Universal History Archive/Getty Images; p. 91 File:Mosaic of St. Justin Martyr, Mount of the Beatitudes.jpg/Wikimedia Commons; p. 93 Universal History Archive/UIG/Getty Images; pp. 99, 100 Look and Learn/Bridgeman Images; p. 103 Steve Geer/iStockphoto.com; p. 109 Leonid Andronov / Shutterstock.com; p. 112 File:The first Ecumenical Council - Google Art Project.jpg/Wikimedia Commons.

Printed in the United States of America

# Contents

# Humble Beginning

Of the world's major religions, Christianity currently enjoys special status as the largest. As of 2010, approximately 2.2 billion people, about a third of the entire world's population, identified as Christian. (By comparison, the world's second-largest religion, Islam, counted nearly 1.6 billion adherents, though it is expected to surpass Christianity within the next few decades.) There are Christians on every continent in nearly every country, from the wealthy states of Western Europe to the developing countries in Central and South America.

Christianity's predominance is impressive, considering its history. Founded by a carpenter-turned-radical named Jesus, probably born between 6 BCE and 4 CE, Christianity largely grew out of the teachings of a man who many contemporaries imagined to be just one of many Jewish prophets preaching in Judaea, which was at the time considered the boondocks of the Roman Empire. During his lifetime, Jesus assembled a

*Opposite:* Members of the world's largest religion pack this church in Marseille.

handful of adherents known as **apostles** or disciples. Largely drawn from the dregs of society, Jesus's followers harbored an intense devotion to their master. These followers considered Jesus to be the **Messiah**, a savior that had been prophesied for centuries in the Jewish religion. Many took to calling him *Christos*, or **Christ**, a Greek word for "anointed one."

Jesus himself lived only until his early thirties before he was executed by Pontius Pilate, the Roman prefect of Judaea, for charges related to sedition. Jesus was neither the first nor the last religious radical to be tortured and executed by the Romans. For the next several centuries, the group of followers Jesus had inspired, increasingly known as Christians, or those who follow Christ, came to be targeted by the Roman government for a variety of reasons: political expediency, moral outrage, or even psychological mania. However, this religion that had in large part been the result of the **persecution** of one man only seemed to grow stronger as the group persecution wore on. Far from quashing Christianity, the Romans only seemed to mint more Christians following in the footsteps of the martyrs that had gone before them.

Eventually, the Romans came to tolerate this determined cult within their borders. After Emperor Constantine himself converted to Christianity in 312 CE, Christianity enjoyed official acceptance and eventual adoption by the state. Indeed, Christianity would prove to have greater staying power than even the powerful Roman Empire, which collapsed before the end of the millennium.

The reported site of the birth of Jesus is marked by the Church of the Nativity in Bethlehem in the West Bank.

# ONE

# The Roots of Christianity

The Christians were a unique group of people in the ancient world. They in many ways resembled so-called personality cults, of which there were many. As the name suggests, personality cults grew up around particularly charismatic individuals, who often preached about new ways of living guaranteed to bring one of a number of boons: happiness, peace, wealth, and so on. In the case of the Christians, that magnetic person was a carpenter from the small town of Nazareth named Yeshua (Joshua), later known as Jesus. Jesus's followers took to calling him the Christ, the one anointed as if a king. They believed him to be the Son of God, at the same time human and divine, and born on earth to save humanity from spiritual transgressions called sins. However, Christ's followers did not call themselves Christians, as they were themselves practicing members of a religion known as Judaism. "Christianity" as a religion arose some

Jesus's radical political and spiritual teachings led him to be executed by the Roman Empire.

time after, out of the need to distinguish followers of Jesus from mainstream Judaism.

## Pre-Christianity

Well before Christianity's founder, Jesus of Nazareth, was even born, the philosophical, historical, and political circumstances that would come to shape the early religion had already been in flux for centuries. It is important to remember that Christianity did not arise out of a cultural vacuum. Just as organized Christianity as a separate religion did not really come into its own until sometime after the time of Jesus Christ, its philosophical heritage also dates back well before the birth of Jesus. The land where Christianity was born, known as Judaea, located in modern-day Israel and Palestine, was—then as now—a volatile cultural melting pot characterized by the presence of several cultures at any given time, each vying for control.

These cultures, including those of the Jews, the Greeks and Macedonians, and the Romans, each had their own religious beliefs and government structures, and these were often opposed to those of the other groups. Thus, peace in the area depended on a delicate balancing of ethnic independence for the subjects and political authority of the colonizers. More often than not, that balancing act often tipped toward the side of open conflict. Understanding this cultural crucible, several millennia in the making, helps to shed light on the unique circumstances that allowed an enigmatic prophet's radical message to resonate with a diverse group of people, as well as their later experience of persecution.

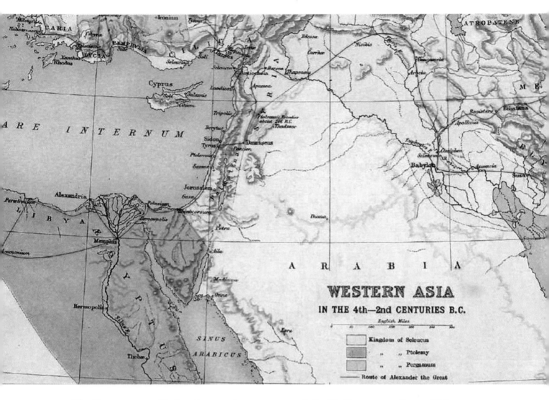

The Roman-controlled region on the east coast of the Mediterranean Sea, which included Judaea, was considered a cultural backwater at the time of Christ.

## The Jews

Christianity began in a place on the eastern shore of the Mediterranean Sea, not far from Mesopotamia, commonly called the "birthplace of civilization." Scholars refer to this area generally as the Near East, but the land itself has gone by many names throughout history. Long before Christianity, the land was called Canaan. Later it was reclassified into two separate places, Palestine and Israel, which persist today. To one group of people, this land is the "Promised Land," given to their forefathers long ago by an all-powerful God.

These people are called the Jews, in reference to the land where they first came from, named Judah (in Greek, Judaea), though they are alternatively referred to as Israelites (after their land, Israel) or Hebrews (after their language, Hebrew).

Jews are both a cultural group and members of a shared religion, called Judaism. Judaism is unique among the world's ancient religions because it was the first to profess **monotheism**, or the belief that there is only one God. Until that point, ancient religions all believed in **polytheism**, the presence of a multitude of gods, each of whom usually governed one aspect of nature and human life in a complex hierarchy. Another distinguishing feature of Judaism is the belief that the one true God is invested in the Hebrews, referred to as his "Chosen People." He has not only reserved a place in his world for them (the "Promised Land"), but also directly engages with the Jews and actively participates in historical events. In contrast, most religions contemporary with the ancient Jews believed that their gods were at best ambivalent toward humanity and at worst actively manipulative or scornful of it. Therefore, these gods had to be pacified with religious rituals.

The history of the Jews is recounted in their sacred books, known collectively as the **Tanakh**. The Tanakh consists of several parts. The first and most important of these is the **Torah**, also known as the Pentateuch, which is Greek for "five scrolls." The first five books of the Hebrew Bible comprise the Torah: Genesis, Exodus, Leviticus, Numbers, and Deuteronomy. Genesis, the first book, begins with an account of how God created the seas, the land, the heavens, and the sun and stars from nothing. From there, he populates the world with sea creatures, then birds and land animals, and at last the first man, Adam, whom God breathes life into, and the first woman, Eve, whom God fashions from Adam's rib. He makes both in his own image. All is well in the world until Adam and Eve disobey God's order to keep away from the Tree of Knowledge of Good and Evil. Seduced by a serpent, the two bite into a fruit from the tree and discover shame at being naked. God decrees that for Adam and Eve, their lives will no longer be as easy and free as they had been. Instead, Adam is cursed to toil in the dirt to grow food, and Eve must suffer pain from childbirth. To Christians adopting this creation story, Adam and Eve's transgression is called original sin, a hereditary state of imperfection that is remedied through **baptism**, an initiation ritual in which an individual is ritually bathed in blessed waters, signifying rebirth.

After Adam, the Torah describes the lives of several figures who prove instrumental to defining Judaism. Of these, perhaps the most influential are Abraham, whose name in Hebrew means "father of multitudes," and Moses. Accounts of Abraham's life go a long way to outlining the promises God makes to the Jews, which are known as **covenants**. At one point, a vision of God appears to Abraham, saying that his descendants will be as numerous as the stars and that they shall have a land of their own. This land, situated between Egypt and the Euphrates River, is Israel. Later in Genesis, God puts Abraham's faith to the test. For much of his life, Abraham did not have a child with his wife, Sarah, until the birth of his son Isaac, which Abraham took to be a blessing from God. However, when Isaac had grown, God said to

Abraham that he must take Isaac into the wilderness and kill him as a sacrifice to God. Though it pained Abraham to do so, he accepted. Just as he was about to kill his son, however, an angel appeared to him and said that it was a test and that Abraham had passed. Abraham was allowed to keep his son.

Though God's Chosen People, the Jews were not without their suffering. Alongside the promises to Abraham, Genesis 15: 13-14 also notes that God said to him: Know for certain that your descendants shall be aliens in a land not their own, where they shall be enslaved and oppressed for four hundred years. But I will bring judgment on the nation they must serve, and in the end they will depart with great wealth.

That land was Egypt, to which the Israelites traveled some time after Abraham's death. There, they became enslaved by the pharaoh and subjected to harsh and often draconian laws. Among the many laws the Hebrews suffered under, one decreed that every male child be drowned. One Jewish family tried to rescue their newborn son from the law by placing him in a basket to float down the Nile River. The child's name was Moses.

Moses was eventually discovered by the pharaoh's daughter, who took him into the palace and raised him as her own. Despite growing up in the lap of luxury, Moses nevertheless had a strong sense of justice and was repulsed by the treatment of his people. One day, Moses killed an Egyptian who was beating a Jew, and he was forced to flee the country. He settled in Midian, located on the Sinai Peninsula, east of Egypt, where he married and had children. One day when he was tending sheep on the slopes of Mount

Horeb (Mount Sinai), God appeared to him in the form of a burning bush and commanded him to return to Egypt and liberate the Hebrews. Moses obeyed, but the pharaoh refused to let the Jews go. In response, Moses, with God's authority, unleashed ten plagues on the Egyptians, culminating in the slaughter of every firstborn son in Egypt at the hands of an angel of death. Eventually, the Hebrews escaped, but they wandered in the desert for forty years before reaching their Promised Land. Along the way, the Jews wavered in their faith that God would deliver them and turned toward the worship of a golden calf reminiscent of the gods of Egypt. When Moses heard of this, he was furious and destroyed the calf.

The worship of the golden calf was among the first of many instances where the Jews turned away from God, suffered because of it, and were beseeched by a divine figurehead to repent and obey God once more. In fact,

Judaism has a long history of religious prophets, such as Jeremiah (*right*), who foretold of suffering for the Jewish people and begged them to change their ways.

# Christianity and Judaism

Christianity's ties with Judaism are numerous and complex. After all, Jesus Christ was himself born into a Jewish family in a Jewish part of the world, practiced in the synagogues (Jewish places of worship), and all of his early followers were themselves Jewish. As such, Christians also share the belief in one all-powerful God with interest in the fate of humanity. In fact, Christians believe that their God and the God of Judaism are one and the same. Lastly, Christianity and Judaism are so closely linked historically and religiously that **sects** of Christianity later adopted the Tanakh into their own Bible, albeit in varying degrees of completion. Christians refer to this collection of books as the **Old Testament**.

Given that Christianity grew out of Judaism, why is it that the two remain distinct religions? This question has historically been a thorny one. Once Christianity became a powerful religion that eventually dwarfed Judaism in number of adherents, that very question was posed to the Jewish people. Unfortunately, religious integrity on the part of the Jews often resulted in persecution at the hands of Christians dissatisfied with the reluctance of the Jews to convert to their religion. Thus, it is important to tread carefully when addressing this question, and it should be considered only with tolerance in mind.

In very broad terms, the reason for the distinction between Christians and Jews arises primarily through the interpretation of Jesus. To Christians, Jesus represents the fulfillment of the messianic prophecies contained in the Old Testament because he is a spiritual savior who cleanses the people of their sins. Jews, meanwhile, cannot believe that Jesus is the Messiah because their Messiah is not a spiritual savior but a political one. In other words, the distinction arises from the difference between Jesus as a spiritual champion and the Messiah as an earthly one. The Jewish prophets specify that the Messiah will accomplish real political goals, such as the implementation of the laws in the Torah, the unification of Israel, and the end of war in *this* life. Jesus did none of those things and, in fact, said that he was superseding the Torah rather than preserving it. Instead, Jesus promises messianic goals in an *afterlife*, governed by God's law and permeated by spiritual peace.

King David is the model for the Jewish interpretation of the Messiah.

much of the Hebrew Bible is concerned with the accounts of prophets who are delivered to the Jews to encourage them to turn away from immoral practices. According to the Talmud, which documents Hebrew civil and ceremonial laws, there have been twice as many prophets as Israelites who fled Egypt—approximately 2.6 million. However, only those whose messages concerned future generations were recorded in the Bible. In addition to the theme of repentance, many of these prophets mention the coming of a Messiah, a primarily political and military leader descended from the great Jewish king David who will organize all Jews from around the world, secure sovereignty for Israel, institute Torah law, and ultimately, bring world peace.

## The Greeks

The other major cultural influence in the area where Christianity would develop came from across the Mediterranean Sea, on a mountainous peninsula surrounded by hundreds of rocky islands: Greece. The Greek influences in the philosophical tenets and religious vocabulary of Christianity are numerous and can be traced back to its earliest beginnings. After all, the word "Christianity" itself comes from an honorific Greek term that was ascribed to Jesus: *christos*, meaning "anointed one." Greek also makes an appearance in Christian iconography, from the symbol of the *ichthys*, or "fish" (see chapter 3), to the conception of Jesus as the *logos*, or "word," of God, in other words, the message and the story communicated from God. The oldest known manuscripts of the oldest **Gospels**, those books in the Christian canon recounting Jesus's life, were written in Greek. The reason for this choice on the part of the Gospel writers, Mark and Matthew, is simple: to reach the widest audience, it helps to communicate in the most widely known language. In the case of the early Christians, that was Greek.

The collection of loosely affiliated city-states that comprised Greece had had contact with the lands to the east of the Mediterranean for several millennia before the birth of Jesus as a result of trade, especially with the Egyptians and the Phoenicians, who occupied the coastal lands of modern-day Israel, Palestine, Lebanon, and Syria. The archaic Greeks incorporated many aspects of ancient Near Eastern cultures into their own, including many mythological ideas about religious practices, as well as art from Egypt. For example, at about the time the Greeks first made contact with Egypt, Greek pottery and sculpture started to reflect the sort of relief statues that Egyptian artists had been crafting.

Perhaps the largest cultural import, though, was the Phoenician system of syllabic writing. Until that time, practically every system of writing was pictographic. Pictographic writing systems, such as the Egyptian hieroglyphics, required that every word be represented by a single corresponding symbol that stood for that word and none else. This meant that written language consisted of an incredibly complex and broad collection of symbols that required specialized knowledge to practice. The Phoenicians made an astounding leap in technology by devising the precursor to the alphabet. Their system was based not on individual words but the sounds of words. So, for example, rather than knowing a special symbol for the word "boat," a Phoenician could break the word down into its corresponding sounds and syllables, which each had a symbol that could be reused for other words with the same sounds. This drastically reduced the number of symbols a person needed to know in order to write; rather than a scribe recalling one intricate pictogram to represent a word, a person could break that word down into its corresponding syllables. Additionally, this allowed people to record words not in their own language. Whereas a pictorial script would be at a loss to document a foreign word, an alphabetic script only had to record the sounds being made. This advancement proved an invaluable tool to the Phoenician traders traveling across the Mediterranean. When the Greeks, traders and adventurers themselves, caught wind of the Phoenician script, they adopted it and improved on it by appropriating some of the existing symbols for vowels used in their own language.

The historical, literary, political, and philosophical effects stemming from development of a simple alphabet by the Greeks cannot be overstated. At home, it democratized written language; no longer was writing a specialized knowledge that required years of training. Common Greeks could now learn the alphabet and begin reading and writing. Soon, the Greeks turned their considerable writing technology to areas of life outside of trade and economic transactions. Individuals began documenting their own ideas and feelings and reading those of others, leading to the development of poetry and philosophy.

Among the many philosophers that Greek culture nurtured was Plato. He was born in the city-state of Athens, the undisputed center of Greek philosophy and art, around 428/7 BCE, and he died around 348/7 BCE. Plato made several arguments that would go a long way toward shaping Christianity. The first of these is his famous "Allegory of the Cave," which he wrote about in his seminal treatise *The Republic*. According to Plato, humanity's experience is like that of prisoners chained in a cave and facing a wall. Behind them is a fire, and between the prisoners and the fire is a path where people hold objects. The light from the fire projects the shadows of those objects onto the wall before the prisoners, and those holding them call out the names of the things they are holding. Thus, the "reality" the prisoners experience is merely shadows and echoes bouncing off the walls of a darkened cave. However, when the prisoners are released, they are blinded by the real sun's light, and the objects they see around them seem less real. Thus, to Plato, reality consists of "Forms," divine truths that cannot be comprehended by humans, and the shadows cast by those Forms, which we can grasp and consider reality, are not themselves real.

The second philosophy of Plato's that directly affected Christian perceptions of the world was his thoughts on the nature of the divine, which stood in stark opposition to the more common beliefs shared among the Greeks. Within the Greek pantheon, there are numerous gods, goddesses, and demigods. These divine beings more often than not seem to share more in common with humans. In the myths of ancient Greece, it is clear that each god has his own motivations, and these frequently manifest in behavior that is far from virtuous and usually outrageous. The Greek creation myth is full of incest, infanticide, and fratricide. Later stories revolve around infighting and bickering among the Olympians, as well as lust and wrath directed at humans. Zeus, for example, is the king of the Greek gods. Although married to Hera, goddess of women and marriage, Zeus frequently has extramarital relations with human women, only some of which are consensual. The two have a rocky relationship, to say the least. Hera, for her part, is often jealous and vengeful toward the women with whom Zeus has such affairs. In one instance, Hera tricks a human woman with whom her husband has had an affair to ask her lover to reveal himself in his full glory, which kills her. Elsewhere, Hera takes her anger out on the product of one of Zeus's affairs, Hercules. Shortly after the demigod is born, Hera sends two poisonous snakes to kill the infant. Hercules, even as a child, manages to strangle the snakes with his bare hands, but Hera isn't done with him yet. Once Hercules has grown, married, and had children, Hera inspires madness in him, and he ends up slaughtering his own family.

To Plato, this concept of the divine as fickle, passionate, and changeable was completely at odds with reason. Instead, he argued, the divine, being infinite and lasting, should be characterized by qualities that support its nature. Among these qualities is perfect oneness: the divine should be contained within itself. The alternative is the pantheon of imperfect gods working in opposite and therefore counterproductive ways.

While it is easy to see how this conception of divinity affected later Christian conceptions of one perfect God, Plato's theology nevertheless argued that divinity must be

The Greek and, by extension, Roman pantheon includes a variety of gods and goddesses who often behave dreadfully. Here, the goddess Hera sends snakes to kill the infant demigod Hercules, the illegitimate child of her husband, Zeus.

passionless. Because emotions change, and the divine is permanent and perfect, there is no room for passion in Plato's understanding. After all, to Plato, love is just the opposite of hate, sympathy the opposite of spite. Thus, while Plato had a sizable effect on shaping the intellectual world that could give rise to Christianity, many Christians perceived his worldview as inaccurate. Nevertheless, the discussion about the nature of reality that was driven by the early Greek philosophers, as well as the qualities of the divine, was already circulating around the ancient world before the birth of Jesus.

## The Hellenistic World

Greek intellectual thought and political organization was introduced by force to the ancient Near East, ironically, by a people who were not from Greece. In the middle of the fourth century BCE, King Philip II of Macedon, a state located to the north of mainland Greece in the Balkans, was envious of Greek culture and decided to lead a campaign to conquer the Peloponnese and incorporate it into Macedonia. In 338 BCE, Philip won a decisive victory against a combined force of allied Greek city-states at Chaeronea. Philip's reign over Greece was not long, however, as just four years later, one of his bodyguards murdered him. Philip's almost twenty-year-old son Alexander assumed the throne.

Alexander benefitted greatly from his father's love for Greek culture and was tutored from a young age by the great Athenian philosopher Aristotle, himself a pupil of Plato. Alexander continued his father's legacy of expansion to unprecedented lengths, conquering enormous tracts of land in the Balkans, the Near East, North Africa, and even India, and toppling the great kingdoms of Egypt and Persia along the way. For this he became known as Alexander the Great. Along the way, Alexander instituted Greek culture in places where its influence had previously been minimal. He founded cities and rechristened existing ones, constructing temples and theaters in the Greek style. Many of these cities he named Alexandria in honor of himself. Among these was Alexandria, situated at the mouth of the Nile in Egypt, whose vast library was renowned the world over. The spread of Greek culture that Alexander drove ushered in the beginning of what historians call the **Hellenistic** period.

Alexander's thirteen-year campaign came to an end in 323 BCE, when he died at the age of thirty-two. The enormous empire quickly fragmented without the dynamic

**Alexander the Great (*left of center*) proved a dynamic and powerful military leader.**

leadership of Alexander the Great. Each of Alexander's top generals divvied the spoils among themselves, with Seleucus I Nicator staking claim to the lands of the Near East from Anatolia to Pakistan. However, the parts of Alexander's empire proved to be weaker than the whole. The Seleucid Empire, as it became known, slowly eroded as a result of civil war among Seleucus's heirs. Furthermore, the vastness of the empire meant that the Seleucids were overextended. Several ethnic groups at the edges of the nation broke off, such as the Bactrians and the Parthians. The ultimate end of the Seleucid Empire came in the second century BCE, when a rival nation with ambitions of conquest similar to that of Alexander marched into Seleucid territory: Rome.

## The Historical Jesus

For all the talk of Jesus's divinity, the general consensus is that he was a real, historical person born into the circumstances of cultural flux between East and West. However, it is at times difficult to parse the historical facts of Jesus's life from the spiritual. For fifty years after the birth of Jesus, there is not a word written about him or any of his followers. In the fifty years after that, certain Christians, writing under the names Mathew, Mark, Luke, and John, began documenting the life of Christ in what are known as the Gospels. (The word "Gospel" is a bastardization of the Anglo-Saxon word "Godspell," or "good news," in reference to the idea that the Gospels documented the arrival of Christ, the savior of mankind.) The Gospels, however, are far from purely biographical accounts of Jesus's life. It is unlikely that the Gospel writers knew Jesus. It was common practice during the time of the writing of the **New Testament** for authors to use a secretary to take dictation or for editors to compile stories related by a person. Historians agree that the earliest Gospel was written by Mark around 70 CE, although the so-called "synoptic Gospels," which comprise those of Mark, Matthew, and Luke, may have all relied on a common source containing Jesus's sayings. Evidence of this source, known as the "Q" source, has been found to date to 40 CE, within a decade of Jesus's death. The last Gospel, that of John, was written around the turn of the first century by John the Evangelist, and is thematically very different from its predecessors.

Taken together, the Gospels constitute the most complete account of the historical Jesus available. According to Matthew and Luke, Jesus was born in Bethlehem, a town in Palestine south of Jerusalem, to parents Mary and Joseph. Jesus's mother was from Nazareth, and his family members were peasant farmers and craftsmen from that town, in the province of Galilee. Joseph was only Jesus's father in the eyes of the law; according to the Gospels, Mary was a virgin and became pregnant through divine intervention. Joseph is said to be descended from the family of David, who came from Bethlehem. Not much is contained in the Gospels about Jesus's childhood, but according to the Gospel of Luke, Jesus was an unusually bright young boy. At one point, the child Jesus instructs men on matters of religion in the temple.

When he was about thirty years old, Jesus traveled to the desert, where he was baptized by an idiosyncratic prophet and healer named John the Baptist. After that, Jesus began traveling throughout Israel, preaching and performing miracles. Early on, he encountered a fishing boat captained by a man named Peter, who had been struggling to catch anything that day. Jesus encouraged him to cast his nets once more, and when Peter pulled them up, they were so full of fish that his boat nearly sank. Peter took to calling Jesus "Lord," and joined him as the first of his disciples.

## Jesus's Radical Politics

Jesus's travels earned him a number of passionate followers from the lower classes of Jewish society, as well as the ire of representatives of mainstream Judaism. Galilee, his homeland, was well known as the seedbed of rebellion against the Romans, who occupied Israel at the time of Jesus, as well as the Jewish establishment that supported them. Jesus's messages had an unusual ability to mobilize the downtrodden, which threatened both Roman and Jewish rule. Jesus's so-called "Sermon on the Mount" described how "the meek" and "poor in spirit" will someday inherit both "the earth" as well as "the Kingdom of Heaven"—in other words, power previously denied to them. Jesus also preached that the end of the world would come during his followers' lifetime. The unjust political organization of the Romans and their establishment supporters would be soon be overthrown and replaced with the world he had described.

Overall, Jesus's message was similar to those of other itinerant preachers and faith healers practicing in the area at the time, including John the Baptist. The larger the crowds these preachers drew, the more successful they were at spreading their message; however, this also ran the risk of attracting attention from authorities who felt threatened by what was said. John the Baptist was one of the more successful preachers. He questioned the morality of the marriage of King Herod Antipas, who ordered that John the Baptist be decapitated and that his head be presented to his stepdaughter on a platter. Likewise, Jesus's success in collecting followers also made him a target.

In his early thirties, Jesus went to Jerusalem, the capital city, to observe the Jewish holiday of Passover, the Jewish people's liberation from bondage under the Egyptians. His arrival was marked by triumphant celebration on behalf of his followers, who laid palm fronds in his path as he rode a donkey. Those assembled cheered Jesus as either the "Son of David" (Matthew 21:9) or "the one who comes in the name of the Lord" (Mark 11:9). According to Luke, the crowd that had gathered around Jesus in Jerusalem believed that the end of the old world order and the beginning of the Kingdom of God was at hand. All this talk of spiritual salvation was also laced with troubling political undertones of physical and political liberation. This procession into the capital was at the same time a pilgrimage and a march.

As soon as Jesus arrived, he traveled to the Temple, where he proceeded to destroy the stalls of the merchants who had set up in the courtyard to sell animals to be used in sacrifice. The priests asked this rabble-rouser on whose authority he acted. Jesus responded in puzzling parables before saying that the most despised members of society, prostitutes and tax collectors, would find salvation before these keepers of the Temple. At last, Jesus foretold that their Temple would be destroyed (Mark 13:1–2).

Passover fell on a Thursday, and Jesus and his disciples prepared a Passover meal. There, Jesus foretold that one of his disciples would betray him, much to the shock of those gathered around him. The dinner proceeded, however. Despite their objections, Jesus washed the feet of his followers. When they were ready to eat, he took the bread, calling it "my body," as well as the wine, which he called "my blood of the covenant" (Mark 14:22–25). When they had finished, Jesus led his disciples into a garden across a valley to pray.

Early the following morning, Friday, Jesus was seized by Roman guards, who were tipped off to his whereabouts by a disciple named Judas. Jesus was brought before Caiaphas, the high priest of the Temple, and a number of his councilors, known as the Sanhedrin. Caiaphas questioned Jesus about his teachings and whether or not he considered himself to be the Son of God, as his followers were saying. The Gospels vary on the exact wording of Jesus's response, though they all record him at some point saying that he was. Mark and Matthew write that Jesus said he was, while Luke records Jesus as ambiguously implying that he was, saying, "If I tell you, you will not believe" (Luke 22:67).

In any case, it seemed Caiaphas and the Sanhedrin had already decided they must get rid of Jesus. Caiaphas accused him of blasphemy and tore his robes as a sign of mourning. They ordered that Jesus be sent to Pontius Pilate, the Roman prefect who oversaw Palestine, with their recommendation that he be executed. Although Caiaphas seemed ready to remove Jesus, the Gospels of Matthew, Luke, and John present Pontius Pilate as being more suspicious. Blasphemy, though punishable under Jewish law, bore little relevance to the Romans. Although Rome controlled the Near East, their only concern was the payment of tribute and the upholding of order. However, this meant that the Jewish establishment had a great deal of autonomy in their own affairs, and Pilate had some measure of duty to respect the high priest's wishes in the interest of preserving their relationship. Pilate charged Jesus with inciting insurrection, citing an accusation made by Caiaphas that Jesus considered himself to be "King of the Jews" (Mark 15:1–2). Indeed, these charges may not have been far from the mark. Given the number of Jesus's followers, his statement about the destruction of the Temple, his destructive behavior in the market, and the fact that Jerusalem was then packed with pilgrims celebrating Passover, Jesus's execution was a matter of political necessity. After being tortured, Jesus was executed by **crucifixion** at

Jesus Christ was executed in the early 30s CE by means of crucifixion, a punishment common among criminals and political rabble-rousers.

Calvary (Golgotha), located outside Jerusalem, alongside two thieves. When he died several hours later, he was buried in a cave. A large boulder that required several men to move was placed at the entrance to prevent anyone from desecrating Jesus's corpse.

## The Resurrection

Jesus lived and died much like countless other contemporary preachers and rebels: having caused a measurable stir after a brief career of preaching spiritual enfranchisement for those left outside the mainstream religious and political system, he was rounded up and executed with little ceremony. However, unlike those countless others, Jesus found life outside of his death—in one way or another. His followers, temporarily silenced in the face of Jesus's humiliating and traumatic execution, found renewed faith in their Lord's divinity. Jesus's followers began reporting that Jesus had indeed died but was **resurrected**, that they had seen them with their own eyes, and that he returned to earth as proof that the Kingdom of God was at hand.

The historical sources for these claims again lie in the Gospels, and yet again, their details differ. (However, Jesus and his resurrection are mentioned in *Jewish Antiquities*, a history of the Jews published in Rome in the first century by Flavius Josephus). Matthew's Gospel mentions that two of Jesus's female followers, both named Mary, were walking to the tomb when an angel appeared to them. The angel showed them that the tomb was empty and told them to go tell Jesus's disciples, who were hiding in Jerusalem, to go

Reports of Jesus's resurrection were widely circulated around Judaea by his followers.

to Galilee and meet Jesus there. Before reaching Jerusalem, the women encounter Jesus himself, who tells them the same thing. Luke's Gospel, the most similar to Matthew's in its account of Jesus's resurrection, again reports that the women first discovered the empty tomb, but it does not mention an angel directly. Instead, Luke says that two men in dazzling apparel approached them at the tomb and told them of Jesus's resurrection. The Gospel of Mark includes several human encounters with a resurrected Jesus but says nothing about Galilee. John's Gospel, meanwhile, says that Peter and another disciple went to the empty tomb and that after they left, Jesus made an appearance to Mary Magdalene outside the tomb.

While these discrepancies prove frustrating for those trying to create an accurate historical account, it does not seem the early Christians were attempting to propagate a conspiracy about their risen lord. If that were the case, it is likely there would be only one story of Jesus's resurrection dictated by a group of highly organized disciples. What scholars have instead are several accounts with differing details, suggesting that reports of Jesus's death had more organic origins. Regardless, one thing is clear: the disciples and others reported that they had indeed seen a corporeal Jesus, alive and well, a claim that would prove to change the course of history.

| | |
|---|---|
| A | AEDES DIVI IVLII |
| B | AEDES CASTORVM |
| C | SACRA VIA |
| D | ROSTRA |
| E | CLIVOS CAPITOLINV |
| F | BASILICA IVLIA |
| G | AEDES SATVRNI |
| H | AEDES CONCORDIAE |
| I | AEDES VESPASIANI |
| K | AEDES IOVIS |
| L | TABVLARIVM |

# TWO

# Rome and Christianity: A Cultural Clash

**W**hether or not Jesus was actually God is a matter of faith. However, the most historically significant fact that followed Jesus's crucifixion was that the early disciples believed he was God and had defeated death to bring about a spiritual kingdom on earth. Armed with their conviction, they were inspired to spread the *evagellion*, the "good news," of the Christ's death and glorious resurrection. Initially, the disciples were limited linguistically primarily to Palestine. Being commoners, Jesus's original disciples spoke Aramaic, a language spoken as far east as Persia. (Aramaic would later be replaced by Arabic.) However, Christianity found greater success in the lands west of Palestine, in Greece and Rome. How was it that this faith known primarily by Aramaic-speaking commoners managed to find a home in the Greek- and Latin-speaking Europe?

*Opposite*: Rome, shown in this map, was near its peak by the time of Jesus's crucifixion.

## Paul of Tarsus

Christianity's westward spread owes to the work of a man named Paul (Saul in Hebrew), who converted to Christianity after Jesus's crucifixion. Paul was born to a Jewish family in Tarsus, a Near Eastern city in Turkey that was historically part of the Greek world. Additionally, for reasons lost to history, Paul enjoyed privileged status as a Roman citizen. Thus, Paul stood at the intersection of the ancient world's three most important cultures: he was religiously Jewish, intellectually Greek, and legally Roman.

Ironically, Paul belonged to a legalistic sect of Judaism that Jesus frequently criticized, and Paul, in turn, worked hard to root out what the Jews considered the Christian **heresy**. Paul traveled to Jerusalem to study under a famous rabbi and eventually become a rabbi himself, devoted to the Torah and the eradication of Christians. Once, however, when he was traveling to Damascus to speak out against Christians there, he experienced an unexpected conversion. According to Acts, chapter 9, while on his way, Jesus appeared to him in a blinding burst of heavenly light. Paul and his companions were dumbstruck as Jesus asked why Paul was persecuting him. Jesus commanded Paul to go to Damascus and await his instructions. When Paul opened his eyes, he found that he was blind, and his companions led him by the hand to their destination. Paul did not eat for three days until a man to whom Jesus had also appeared came to him, laid his hands on him, and healed him. Paul could again see, and decided to be baptized in the Christian faith.

From then on, Paul began preaching in the synagogues of Damascus that the Christians were not to be persecuted, that they were right, and that the promised Messiah had indeed come. Naturally, the Jewish establishment plotted to rid their temples of this heretic, but Paul escaped the city by having his companions lower him over the walls in a basket.

## Paul and the Spread of Christianity

There are many traditions about how Christianity spread, but there is little historical evidence to trace its exact route. There were small collections of Christians in places like Damascus, Antioch, and Alexandria a few years following Jesus's execution, but how they came to be is unclear. However,

Paul's cultivation of communities throughout the Roman Empire is well documented.

After his conversion and his escape from Damascus, Paul began taking his message west, into Greece and Rome. Fortunately for Paul, he enjoyed relative immunity from prosecution at the hands of local communities by right of his status as a citizen of Rome. Classically trained in Greek rhetoric as a child and versed in Jewish law, he was a skilled debater capable of holding his own against the rabbis and skeptics he encountered along the way. During his travels, he established small communities of new Christians in places like Athens and Corinth in Greece, to whom he frequently addressed letters to inform them of the faith and to encourage them to keep it. Many of these have been collected in the Christian Bible.

As a Jew, Paul preferred to make the local synagogue his first stop in a new town; however, when he was rejected, Paul would reply, "My conscience is clear; now I shall go to the **Gentiles**," and take his message into the public forums (Acts 18:16). Gentiles are non-Jews, and so they include the overwhelming majority of the world's people. The opening up of a faith based on the fulfillment of ancient Jewish prophecies to non-Jews was an unprecedented philosophical development with staggering historical connotations. Now, Christianity was free to welcome the whole world into the fold.

However, opening up Christianity to non-Jews also lead to an identity crisis. Up until this point, the Christians had all been Jews—Jesus was a Jew, the disciples were all Jews, and those they converted were all Jews. If Christianity was not a sect of Judaism, then what was it? Paul journeyed to Jerusalem, where he met with Peter, Jesus's preeminent disciple, to discuss the matter, which centered on **circumcision**. Like baptism in Christianity, circumcision has signified the ritual entry of a male into the Jewish religion since the time of Abraham; however, it bore little appeal to the Gentiles, many of them middle aged, whom Paul was converting—for obvious reasons. If Gentiles were required to be circumcised before entering into Christianity, it's likely Christianity would lose many of its converts. Ultimately, Peter and Paul declared that it would not be required, much to the excitement of the converts. The decision was a boon to Paul's view of what the new religion should be: not one for a group of people but for the world.

Paul proved to be such an effective evangelist that the Jewish authorities in Jerusalem grew fearful enough of Christianity that they arrested him. Acts quotes the Jews as saying, "We found this man to be a pest; he creates dissension among Jews all over the world and is a ringleader of the sect of the Nazarenes [Christians]" (Acts 24:5). Paul's Roman citizenship entitled him to a proper Roman trial, of which he took advantage. Thus, he was taken to Rome, the heart of the empire. The book of Acts, which documents Paul's travels abroad, ends without an account of Paul's trial or death. However, given the state of Rome in the mid-first century CE, it is unlikely he fared well.

# Rome's Beginnings:
# A Story of Violence

From the beginning, Rome had a culture built on brutality. The stories people tell about themselves offer important insights into their character and how they view the world. In the case of the Romans, those stories demonstrate a pattern of politically motivated violence that was not only common in Roman history but generally accepted and even celebrated. Once Christianity, whose central figure met his death passively, penetrated the western parts of the Roman Empire in the early centuries CE, they combined in explosive ways.

Rome had always had a history of political turbulence, where coups were the norm and disputes were settled by the sword more often than not. Even its mythological founding has traditionally been steeped in blood. According to legend, the Italian peninsula, known in the ancient world as as Latium, was dominated by a city named Alba Longa, which was ruled by a king named Numitor. Numitor was usurped by his younger brother Amulius, who sent his brother into exile and killed all of Numitor's male heirs to consolidate his power. He also forced Numitor's daughter, Rhea Silvia, to become a Vestal Virgin, one of an order of priestesses sworn to chastity and tasked with keeping a sacred fire devoted to the goddess Vesta alight. As the story goes, Rhea Silvia became pregnant with two twin boys by either Heracles (Hercules), the legendary demigod renowned for his unmatched strength, or Mars, the Roman god of war. According to the Roman author Livy, however, it is more likely she was raped by an unknown human man. Amulius discovered Rhea Silvia to be pregnant; however, rather than execute her as was customary for Vestal Virgins who broke their vow of chastity, he imprisoned her and allowed her to give birth. Amulius believed the stories being told about the children's parentage and feared reprisal from their divine father should he kill the children himself, so after the children were born, Amulius ordered a servant to take them into the wilderness and abandon them to die of exposure. Once the servant reached the Tiber River, located in central Italy, he took pity on the children. Rather than abandon them, the servant decided to place them in a basket and float them downriver in the hope that they would be discovered and cared for.

The river god Tibernus carried the twins to safety, depositing them within the roots of a tree along the river. There they were discovered by a *lupa*, or wolf, who nursed them. Eventually, the twins were taken in by a shepherd and named Romulus and Remus. When the twins had grown, the shepherding families battled with King Amulius, who took Remus as a prisoner. Romulus, in response, organized a band of armed men to rescue his brother. They returned to Alba Longa, killed King Amulius, and reinstated their grandfather Numitor.

In 753 BCE, Romulus and Remus endeavored to found their own city. They each chose a spot along the Tiber, where their basket had been discovered, though they couldn't agree on where to place their city. Remus preferred the Aventine Hill and Romulus wanted the Palatine Hill. They decided that they would leave their decision in the hands of fate, using a mystical rite known as **augury**. The two sat on their respective hills, looking for a sign. Remus was the first to spot six eagles congregating on the Aventine, but shortly after, Romulus saw twelve eagles. Remus believed his was the better sign because it came first, but Romulus disagreed, saying that his, though second, had twice as many eagles. In the end, they began constructing their cities on opposite hills.

When Romulus began to build a wall around his city, Remus jeered him, saying that it was much too short. To prove his point, Remus jumped the walls, mocking his brother as he did. In a rage, Romulus killed his own brother, saying, "So perish every one that shall hereafter leap over my wall," and thereby consolidated his power. He named the city Roma (Rome) in his own honor.

Romulus's murder of his brother isn't the only dark chapter in the city's mythological beginnings. When Romulus had founded Rome, he had with him only those shepherds whom he had led to rescue Remus, along with some exiles, refugees, and escaped criminals fleeing nearby villages and cities in search of **amnesty** within the new city's walls. The overwhelming majority of this ragtag collection of outcasts were men. Romulus realized that there were too few women to support a city's population, so he devised a plan to bring more women into the city. Romulus invited the neighboring Latin and Sabine people to the city for a festival. The Latins and Sabines accepted, bringing their families with them. Once the Romans had filled the Sabine men with wine, they each grabbed a woman, dragging them into their homes, and locked the Latin and Sabine men out of the city. The

*The Intervention of the Sabine Women* was painted in 1799 by Jacques-Louis David.

event became known as the Rape of the Sabine Women. Once the Latins and Sabines had sobered up, they were outraged at the kidnapping of their sisters and daughters. The Latins went to war with the Romans and were soundly defeated. As the Sabines and the Romans prepared for war, the kidnapped women begged for peace between the two. The Sabines and Romans formed a truce. The Romans were allowed to keep the stolen women, and the Sabines were largely welcomed into the fold of Rome.

## Reading the Founding Story

It's difficult to parse where these stories stray from the historical into the mythological. Many of the more legendary aspects, such as the paternity of Romulus and Remus tracing back to

Mars or Hercules, have logical explanations. Regardless, these stories were commonly known among the Romans. As foundational myths, they demonstrate what sorts of qualities the Romans thought were integral to their identities. The first of these is the idea that the Romans were destined to control the land along the Tiber. Romulus and Remus's arrival at the spot where Rome would eventually be founded is improbable, to say the least. It depended on the unexpected charity of a servant and the unlikely survival of two infant boys traveling alone in a basket on a dangerous river in the wilderness. On top of that, the spot of the city itself, the Palatine Hill, was marked with an auspicious sign of twelve eagles, suggesting that the location was pinpointed by the gods. While the city of Rome itself would expand beyond the Palatine, encompassing all seven of the hills surrounding the Tiber, and the empire of Rome would later stretch from Britain to Tunisia and from Spain to Persia, the Palatine would remain the city's heart, eventually serving as the home for the future emperors.

The second quality integral to the Roman persona as indicated by the founding story is Rome's inclination toward war and bloodshed. According to the story, Romulus and Remus are the sons of either Mars, the god of war, or Hercules, the demigod of legendary strength, and the two were literally raised by a wolf. In that way, Romulus and Romans in general as his "offspring" are naturally inclined toward violence. This violence makes an appearance at several points in the story, but especially in the Sabine episode. When faced with the possible collapse of Roman society, Romulus leads an effort to mass kidnap the marriageable women of neighboring villages. When met with resistance from the Latins, the Romans go to war in defense of their crime and utterly destroy the opposition. Peace only comes to the land once the Sabines, the aggrieved party, capitulate and ultimately incorporate themselves within Roman society.

Violence skews specifically toward the political in Rome's founding story. At several points in the legend, political discrepancies arise and are answered with violent overthrow. The story is at its core one of power and nation building. It begins with the expulsion of a sitting king and the bloody execution of the king's heirs, a politically motivated act intend to consolidate power. Later on, the pretender himself is killed and the king restored by Romulus and Remus, but not before Remus is taken as a prisoner in what is essentially a bureaucratic land-use conflict between the shepherds and the king. From there, Romulus and Remus go on to found their own cities and institute their own governments there. After Romulus has established the limits of his city, Remus's jumping of the walls equates to a political transgression (albeit a juvenile one), which Romulus answers with uncompromising force.

These themes of racial destiny and violence, especially politically motivated violence, constitute the building blocks of the Roman identity. The Roman way illustrated in the story of Romulus is not simply limited to the **apocryphal** founding of the city; rather, these characteristics frequently recur throughout Rome's documented history. Understanding these principles also goes a long way toward illuminating a discussion of a unique part of that long history: the treatment of the Christians.

# Christians in Rome

Ironically, the culture that was largely incompatible with Christianity's precepts also made the religion's rise possible. The *Pax Romanum* (Peace of Rome) that accompanied the emperor Octavian Augustus's defeat of his rivals in a civil war following the assassination of Caesar at about the time of Jesus's birth, manifested in a relatively tranquil empire. Trade flourished along the Mediterranean Sea, where a long history of piracy had all but concluded, as well as on Rome's superb infrastructure of roads that linked nearly all corners of the empire. (The roads built by the ancient Romans were in fact so sophisticated and well built that many still exist in pristine condition today, several millennia after they were first built. By comparison, modern roads, constructed mostly of blacktop pavement, require regular resurfacing every decade or so.)

Christian communities in Rome predate Paul's arrival in the mid-60s CE, though like those that formed outside of Paul's travels, it is unclear how these Christians came to reside in Rome. One theory is that they were imported as slaves from Palestine. (Rome at the time sponsored a booming slave trade, circulating prisoners of war, criminals, and political captives around the empire to serve as household attendants, gladiators, and so on.) Some Christians may have converted after hearing stories about the new religion from traders traversing the Mediterranean.

However they got to Rome, the Christians produced a steady stream of converts, despite the increasing amount

# Founding Parallels

The story of Rome's founder bears several fascinating resemblances to those of seminal figures from both Judaism and Christianity: Moses and Jesus of Nazareth. Like Romulus and Remus, Moses, born as an enslaved Jew in Egypt, was abandoned as an infant to float in a basket down the Nile River to escape retribution at the hands of a power-mad ruler. Likewise, shortly after he was born, Jesus also underwent a similar exodus, at least in the Gospel according to the apostle Matthew. In his case, Jesus, along with his mother Mary and father Joseph, traveled to Egypt to escape King Herod in Judaea. Herod had heard rumors about a boy king born in Israel who was destined to free his people, and he endeavored to kill every recently born boy in his kingdom. (Of course, given that Matthew's is the only Gospel in which this particular moment of Jesus's life is recounted, it is possible that it is less biographical as much as it is an allusion intended to draw a connection between Moses, savior of the Jews in Egypt, and Jesus, savior of mankind).

Lastly, all three—Romulus, Moses, and Jesus—eventually return to their birthplaces—Alba Longa, Egypt, and Israel, respectively. There, they organize followers—shepherds, the Jews, and all humanity—and liberate their people from the power of unjust rulers—King Numitor, the pharaoh, Pilate and the Roman Empire. The comparison is far from perfect, however. Romulus, himself a worldly ruler, achieved his ends through bloodshed, while Moses and Jesus wielded power originating from God.

of criticism and false accusations constantly lobbed in their direction. Christianity provided spiritual and physical security, the latter of which appealed especially to the lower classes of Roman society. Charity was one of the primary obligations Jesus placed on his disciples, and early Christian communities worked to alleviate the suffering of their poorer members. Deacons, one of three ministries organized by the early Christian Church, were expressly tasked with this duty. Additionally, the Christian Church eased anxiety over one of the most important (and expensive) facets of ancient life: burials. At the time, most ancient people believed the fate of their soul was in part determined by the treatment of their body after death, and there were a large number of people living in ancient Rome who did not have the means to pay for their funeral. Poor Christians, however, could expect their community to help pay for a proper interment.

## The Problem with Christians

As communities of Christians grew large enough to raise notice, they earned a negative reputation because of their unusual beliefs and practices. For one thing, the Christians were in practically every way "other." Socially, Christians were like any number of groups of poor foreigners that the dignified Romans considered barbarians and treated as second-class citizens. However, Christianity struck an even deeper chord with the Romans: other groups may not be Roman, but Christians seemed to be decidedly and deliberately un-Roman, even anti-Roman. For one thing, many early Christians, especially those in Rome itself, spoke Greek, not Latin, and Greek remained the official language of the church in Rome until the third century. Rome had for centuries harbored a complicated relationship with Greece: Rome suffered from a cultural inferiority complex, adopting much of Greece's religion, philosophy, architecture, and political organization; however, this sense of inferiority also caused an inverse hatred for all things Greek.

Besides the Christians being so foreign, the Romans also took issue with the religion's principles. Christianity's tenets and rituals are relatively commonplace all over the world today, but to the ancient world they appeared fundamentally alien and bizarre. After all, Christianity's central figure, considered by its adherents to be God, died an agonizing and humiliating death alongside common criminals in an unimportant corner of the empire. Compared to the illustrious gods of Greece and Rome, who wield the powers of nature and use humans as playthings, or even the God of Judaism, who despite his compassion for his Chosen People is still all-powerful and at times wrathful, the Christians' faith in Jesus seemed misplaced, even misguided.

The Romans also saw the Christians' rituals to be odd at best and diabolical at worst. The central ritual of Christianity was then known as *agape*, or "Love Feast," which comes from the Greek for "brotherly love." The agape was a communal meal in which the congregation gathered around a priest, who sanctified bread and wine and shared it. The agape was closely modeled after the Passover meal Jesus shared with his disciples the night before his crucifixion. The early Christians gathered for their meal in secret, it seems primarily to evade detection by the authorities. Ironically, this furtiveness also sparked the rampant speculation about its proceedings on behalf of those on the outside.

While there were a number of secret societies and cults operating throughout the empire and within Rome at the time, some of them violent and sexually deviant in nature, the Christian "Love Feast" struck many Romans as morally depraved and diabolical. On the one hand, the Romans believed the name "agape" itself suggested some twisted sexual practice, most likely orgies. There was also a rumor that Christians consumed the flesh and blood of human victims like cannibals. One surviving accusation about Christian rituals comes from the third-century writer Minucius Felix, who claims that his account was taken from Marcus Cornelius Fronto, a Roman speaker and teacher who lived in the second century.

The ritual of communion, of receiving the body and blood of Jesus, fueled speculation among the Romans that Christians were cannibals.

A young baby is covered over with flour, the object being to deceive the unwary. It is then served before the person to be admitted into the rites. The recruit is urged to inflict blows onto it—they appear to be harmless because of the covering of flour. Thus the baby is killed with wounds that remain unseen and concealed. It is the blood of this infant—I shudder to mention it—it is this blood that they lick with thirsty lips; these are the limbs they distribute eagerly; this is the victim by which they seal their covenant …

On a special day they gather in a feast with all their children, sisters, mothers—all sexes and all ages. There, flushed with the banquet after such feasting and drinking, they begin to burn with incestuous passions. They provoke a dog tied to the lamp stand to leap and bound towards a scrap of food which they have tossed outside the reach of his chain. By this means the light is overturned and extinguished, and with it common knowledge of their actions; in the shameless dark with unspeakable lust they copulate in random unions, all equally being guilty of incest, some by deed, but everyone by complicity.

The rumor that Christians ate flesh and blood is based partly in fact, though it is an extreme misrepresentation. Jesus had said at his Last Supper that the bread and wine were his body and blood, given in sacrifice to his disciples. At the Christian agape, the priests recreated this scene, claiming the bread and wine arranged at the altar were changed into the body and blood of Jesus. While later sects of Christianity debated whether or not the blood and wine is indeed transformed into the literal body of Christ, the meal has always consisted of simple bread and wine. The descriptions of incestuous orgies, meanwhile, are completely unfounded, based solely on speculation over the meaning of the term "love feast."

These rumors contributed to a fear of Christians among the Romans. At one point, the Roman historian Suetonius referred to the Christians as "a class of men given to new and wicked superstition."

## Early Christian Symbolism

Adding to the sense of mystery around the Christian religion, the early Christians also devised an arsenal of complex symbols. Symbols have been used by religions since before history to signify a variety of things, such as peace, spiritual balance, power, and so on. Other religious symbols are designed to communicate affiliation or protect secrets to those "in the know," while concealing that information from those outside the religion. In the case of the early Christians, many of these symbols were designed for the latter purpose. This was often done to avoid persecution. However, although these symbols often achieved the goal of keeping knowledge of Christian affiliation out of the hands of the Romans, it had the effect of fueling Roman paranoia about the new cult.

Perhaps the most famous early Christian symbol besides the cross is the *ichthys*, the Greek word for "fish." An ichthys is formed with two curved lines which have the same beginning point and crisscross before their end points, forming a crude fish. There are many examples of early Christian ichthyses graffitied on ancient Roman ruins, and the symbol has found renewed popularity in the form of bumper stickers. Fish were spiritually and economically important to the early Christians. Fish frequently appear in the Gospels. Many of Jesus's disciples were fishermen, whom he called to be "fishers of men" (Matthew 4:19). In the Gospel of Matthew, Jesus performs a miracle in which he feeds five thousand listeners who had gathered around him with five loaves of bread and two fish. Additionally, evidence suggests that the early Christians shared fish, as well as bread and wine, at their meals.

Adding to the complexity of the symbol, the word "ichthys" itself is an anagram, in which each of the letters stands for a certain word. Thus, ichthys stands for the Greek phrase "*Iesos Christos Theou Yios Soter,*" which in English translates into "Jesus Christ, Son of God, Savior." (Once again, the ichthys as a Greek symbol betrayed the early Christians' foreignness to the Romans.)

While the ichthys is relatively simple to grasp, Christians in Rome also engaged in far more complex wordplay. Take the so-called Sator Square for example:

R O T A S
O P E R A
T E N E T
A R E P O
S A T O R

The five words in this five-letter square block are all Latin and generally translates as "The farmer Arepo has a wheel to work"—which is nearly nonsense. However, a closer look reveals a far more complex and multivalent structure at work. First of all, the Sator Square is a palindrome, meaning that it is spelled the same way forward as backward. A still closer look reveals that the word "TENET" appears twice, once in the third line and again read downward in the third letter of each of the words. The two TENETs form a cross and suggest the key to an even deeper meaning. Looking yet more closely, the letters of the square are anagrammatic, meaning that they can be rearranged to form the following:

From a complex word puzzle another complex puzzle is formed. Here, the letters in the Sator Square have been rearranged to form the words *"pater noster"* twice, if the single *N* is shared, as well as two *A*s and two *O*s. In addition to forming a cross, "pater noster" also happens to be Latin for "Our Father," the first two words in the most important

Christian prayer. The *As* and *Os* represent the Greek letters alpha and omega, the first and last letters of the Greek alphabet. Alpha and omega, first and last, are symbolic of Jesus, whom the Christians believe "was" at the beginning and "will be" there at the end of everything.

These are just two of a number of symbols the early Christians used to communicate their faith to one another in the Roman Empire. As in the case of the Sator Square, many of these symbols were deliberately arcane and designed to covertly conceal one's affiliation with the cult of Christianity from those outside, such as the **pagan** Romans. However, while pagans may not have understood these symbols, they felt threatened by their increasing commonness. As has happened countless times throughout history, Roman ignorance of Christian symbols and rituals fueled paranoia and ultimately led to tragedy.

## The Limits of Roman Tolerance

It is important to note that the Roman Empire, like many others empires of the ancient world, actually maintained a policy that was generally tolerant of foreign religions for centuries; to do so was a matter of political necessity when administering an empire that spanned much of the known world and encompassed dozens of ethnic groups and religions. On the one hand, to require each culture to completely abandon its gods and adopt Roman ones would rankle the hearts of Rome's subjects and run the risk of constant rebellion. On the other, Rome didn't care to convert those living within its borders; instead, the Romans were content to leave those lands to their own devices, as long as they kept quiet and paid their taxes.

The Romans did acknowledge, however, that religion also had a political component. A person's religion goes a long way toward forming his identity, his beliefs, and his actions, so while Rome was satisfied to have a variety of religions within its empire, it also sought to mobilize religion in a way that conquered people could identify both with being members of the empire's constituent cultures—Greeks and Egyptians, say—and also subjects of Rome as a whole. Whenever the Romans incorporated a new territory into the folds of the empire, they allowed those conquered to maintain their religions but demanded that they also accept the imperial cult, which held that all Roman emperors—past, present, and future—are gods, and that Roman subjects make regular animal sacrifices to the good health and success of the emperors.

In general, this requirement was manageable for most conquered territories, which were pagan like the Romans— after all, what's adding a few more gods to a pantheon, if only in principle? However, two groups in particular within the Empire refused to make this concession: the Jews and the Christians. Both strictly believed in the presence of one true God, and neither would be brought to worship another, let alone a whole line of emperors who had been subjugating Judaea for centuries. In the case of Judaism, Rome was prepared to make an exception to the requirement, citing Judaism's long, established history. Interestingly, although there were a number of Jewish revolts against Roman rule, which the Romans in turn crushed brutally, the Romans seem to have harbored an unusual respect for Judaism. Judaism enjoyed special status as *religio licita*, "an allowable/lawful religion." (In fact, the Romans even adopted Judaism's seven-day measurement of a week instead of the traditional Roman eight.)

Christianity also enjoyed this benefit by extension for a brief time, but once Christians separated more cleanly from Judaism and became a distinct religion, the expectation was placed on them to adapt to Rome's religious mandate. Christianity became a crime punishable by death, although a pardon was granted to those who adopted the mandate. The Christians were no less opposed to the imperial cult than the Jews were. The Christians, for their part, also viewed the Romans as morally corrupt. In his letters to the Romans, Paul makes it clear that any worship "of an image of mortal man [implying especially the Roman emperors] or of birds or of four-legged animals or of snakes" is an abomination punishable by God's wrath (Romans 1:23). Unfortunately for the Christians, they lacked the same sort of cultural pedigree that the Jews had. Some Christians argued publicly that Christianity, though separate from Judaism, nevertheless shared Judaism's historical and spiritual legacy. This argument failed to convince the Romans, who would not tolerate this strange new cult's audacity to resist Rome's commands.

# THREE

# Pagan Policies of Persecution

By the middle of the first century CE, Christian communities in Rome had grown large enough to garner not only the notice of officials but the animosity of mainstream Roman society. The Roman historian Tacitus, in his book *Annales* documenting the history of the Roman Empire, captured the general opinion of this time: "Their originator, Christ, had been executed in Tiberius' reign by the governor of Judaea, Pontius Pilate. But in spite of this temporary setback the deadly superstition had broken out afresh, not only in Judaea (where the mischief had started) but even in Rome. All degraded and shameful practices collect and flourish in the capital."

The Romans considered Christianity to be, in Tacitus's words, *superstitio* (a superstition), and its adherents were seen as antisocial—literally "against the people"—due to the Christians' practice of withdrawing from public life and obligations in order to have their communal meals.

This painting by Caravaggio depicts the crucifixion of Jesus's chief apostle, Peter.

The Christians were not pitiable but laughable to the Romans. The historian Lucian writes:

> The poor wretches have convinced themselves that they are going to be immortal and live for all time, by worshipping that crucified sophist and living under his laws. Therefore, they despise the things of this world, and consider them common property. They receive these doctrines by tradition, without any definite evidence, so if any charlatan or trickster comes among them, he quickly acquires wealth by imposing upon these simple folk.

At this point, the language of Roman historians clearly bends toward the disapproving, characterizing the Christians as immoral and illogical, but little action was taken about the peculiar new cult. That would soon change with the ascendance of an emperor whose rule can only be characterized as psychopathic and sadistic.

## Nero

In 54 CE, Rome's fifth emperor took the throne: Nero Claudius Caesar Augustus Germanicus, known simply as Nero. Even before Nero became emperor, his path to the throne was coated in blood. His mother, Agrippina the Younger, a great-granddaughter of Rome's first emperor, Octavian Augustus, had great expectations for her son. After her first husband died in 40 CE, Agrippina plotted to marry her uncle Claudius, the sitting emperor. She had her second husband poisoned and orchestrated the murder of Claudius's wife in 48 CE. From there, Agrippina worked to persuade the impressionable and awkward Claudius to disown his own son, Britannicus, and favor her son Nero for succession. Claudius died in 54 CE, most likely poisoned by Agrippina; Agrippina also poisoned Britannicus in 55, as well as her opponents among Claudius's advisors. With the support of the Praetorian Guard, the elite cohort of soldiers feared by even the Roman Senate, Agrippina declared Nero emperor. He was not yet seventeen.

Interestingly, Nero's biographers record the boy emperor's early reign as generous. Nero's government (largely under the direction of Nero's advisors, the Praetorian prefect Sextus Afranius Burrus and philosopher Lucius Annaeus Seneca) banned public spectacles involving bloodshed at the circus and capital punishment. Nero also permitted slaves the right to bring civil complaints in Roman courts against overly cruel masters. He even pardoned those who wrote and plotted against him, an act of mercy uncharacteristic of the Roman line of emperors.

Although Nero's eccentricities skewed toward the beneficent in his teenage years, it seems these and other acts of kindness were early manifestations of a far more troubling mania. While Seneca and Burrus tended to the task of running the government in Nero's stead, they left the boy emperor to his own devices. Once he realized the true extent of his power—that is, that there was no limit—Nero took to satisfying his personal whims. In 59, he sentenced Agrippina to death after seeing his mother fly into a rage over losing control of her son. Nero's order earned the praise of the senators, who saw Agrippina as a bad influence. This seemed to only inflate Nero's sense of self-importance. In 62, to the disapproval to the people, he executed his first wife Octavia, on charges that she had fallen in love with the wife of a senator.

Nero's mania continued to escalate. He fancied himself a poet, musician, actor, and charioteer, and in the late 50s he spent enormous amounts of money to gratify his sense of personal artistic prowess. Sometime between 59 and 60 CE, he began giving public performances, and theaters began allowing him to assume every role in productions. Public opinion sunk even lower, as this was considered to be bad etiquette for a member of the elite.

In July 64, a fire that had started in the Circus Maximus in Rome burned out of control, engulfing practically the entire city in flames. Legend has it that Nero himself started the Great Fire of Rome, but this is doubtful. Nero was in the city of Antium, 38 miles (61 kilometers) south of the capital, when the fire started, and most structures in the crowded city of Rome were built of wood and other combustible materials. However, the rumor spread among Rome's surviving populace that Nero had not only started the blaze but that he gleefully played the lyre and sang "The Sack of Ilium" (a song of his own composition) while he watched it from his palace, an image immortalized by the historian Suetonius.

Nero attempted to salvage public opinion by placing the blame on the Christians. In the *Annales*, Tacitus again comments: "To be rid of this rumor, Nero fastened the guilt on a class hated for their abominations, called Christians by

**Although evidence points to the contrary, many Romans believed that Nero started the Great Fire of Rome himself, to make room for a new palace.**

the populace." Suetonius corroborates Tacitus's evaluation in *Nero*. The Christians made great **scapegoats**. By this point, they were reviled enough that everyday Romans wouldn't care if they were guilty or not, and the size of their communities and their doctrine of passive resistance to persecution meant they would not put up much of a fight.

## The Spectacle of Persecution

Although everyday Romans did not care for Christians, persecution did not necessarily have grassroots support. According to Tacitus, most Romans recognized that Nero was using the Christians as a political diversion to draw attention away from plummeting public opinion: "It was felt that they were being sacrificed to one man's brutality rather than to the public interest," he wrote. Rather than ignite a popular movement against Christians, Nero simply initiated a long history of intermittent and halfhearted persecution of Christians at the hands of publicly embattled emperors for the purposes of political expediency.

"Halfhearted" may describe the mainstream Roman approach to the persecution of Christians, but that was far from the case for the Christians themselves, who were subjected to unimaginable tortures whenever an emperor thought it would serve his ends. Nero made sure the executions of Christians were public events. "Mockery of every sort was added to their deaths," Tacitus writes. "Covered with the skins of beasts, they were torn by dogs and perished; or were nailed to crosses; or were doomed to the flames. Nero threw open his garden for the spectacle and exhibited a show in the circus."

Tacitus describes several appalling means of executing the Christians. Many, like Jesus himself, were crucified, which was so agonizing that the Latin word for crucifixion, *cruciare*, is also the root of the word "excruciating." Crucifixion had been around since the sixth century BCE, well before the ascendance of the Romans, though it was among the most common ways the Romans punished rebels, pirates, and slaves. When the Roman general Marcus Licinius Crassus quashed the slave uprising lead by Spartacus in 71 BCE, he rounded up six thousand survivors and crucified them along the Appian Way, the main thoroughfare into Rome.

Despite the frequency with which the Romans crucified people, it is unclear how exactly crucifixion worked. There has been a large amount of debate among biblical historians and archaeologists over the specific means of crucifixion, the understanding of which has evolved over the decades. The popular conception of crucifixion, represented in countless depictions of Jesus Christ's crucifixion for millennia, suggest that the condemned was scourged or whipped, stripped naked, and forced to carry a wooden T called a cross to the place of execution. From there, the cross would be placed in the ground and the person attached to the cross with nails through the palms or wrists and feet or ankles.

However, historians tend to agree that this image is inaccurate. Evidence suggests that the condemned carried only the crossbeam to the execution location, where fixed poles used in multiple crucifixions stood. According to the ancient Jewish historian Josephus, a shortage of timber, especially in the Near East, required that the posts used in crucifixions had to be recycled to extend their useful life. Once the condemned reached the post, the crossbeam was attached to the top of the pole, and the victim's ankles were nailed to either side of it. Historians disagree whether or not the person's wrists were also nailed or if they were just tied to the crossbeam. It is a moot point, however, as the actual trauma of crucifixion came not from the blood loss stemming from the piercing of hands and feet but from the position of the body. A condemned person's body would be arranged in such an unnatural way that the muscles responsible for breathing would slowly weaken over time. Breathing would grow increasingly labored and at last stop, resulting in a slow and painful asphyxiation.

According to Tacitus, Nero took the horrors of crucifixion one step further. "When the daylight passed away," Tacitus writes, "they [Christians] were used as nighttime lamps." It is unclear whether the Christians who were set on fire were also crucified or if they were simply tied to poles. Even if the Christians were crucified before being burned, it seems likely that many were still alive, considering that the process of crucifixion could take several hours and sometimes days for a person to succumb to asphyxia. Tacitus continues to comment that Nero crucified and burned the Christians in his own imperial garden, which he opened to the public, as well as in the arenas and the Circus Maximus, which was used for horse races. Nero arranged the Christians around the central wall dividing the two sides of the racecourse and rode his chariot among them.

There is little evidence to indicate how many Christians Nero killed during this time period, but it is likely to be at least in the hundreds. Nero also likely executed Paul of Tarsus, who was imprisoned at the time, as well as Peter, who according to legend was condemned to crucifixion but requested that

Of those Christians executed under Nero, a few were used as "lamps" in his courtyard; crucified or just attached to poles, they were burned alive (*right*).

he be placed upside down so that he might not die the same way as Jesus did. Although Nero hoped to dispel the rumor that he had started the fire with an unconscionable public display of brutality, the slaughter did little to change the Roman people's perception of their emperor. In fact, it may have worsened their opinion while sparking something like compassion for the Christians. Tacitus's section on Nero's persecution concludes with the following: "Even though they [the Christians] were clearly guilty and merited being made the most recent example of the consequences of crime, people began to pity these sufferers, because they were consumed not for the public good but on account of the fierceness of one man."

## Martyrs and Saints

In addition to doing little to change public opinion, Nero's persecution also had the unintended consequence of bolstering the Christians' conviction. Rather than cower in fear and hide from the authorities, many saw the executions as a challenge to hold true to their faith—the more horrific, excruciating, and humiliating the ordeal, the better. In hoping to model their lives after Jesus Christ, it made sense that the early Christians desired to model their deaths after Christ's execution as well.

This belief was closely associated with the Kingdom of Heaven, Christianity's conception of the afterlife. Jesus had taught that entrance into God's kingdom was exclusive to those who lived according to his example. Thus, suffering as Jesus did while holding true to the faith was believed to ensure entrance into heaven. This practice came to be known as **martyrdom**, and those who achieved it were called martyrs. The martyrs were measured both by the savagery of their execution and their bravery and dignity in death. Indeed, Christianity's first **saints**, those whom the Catholic Church believes are already in heaven and are therefore worthy of veneration, were all martyrs.

Martyrdom was an appealing fate for many early Christians. The bones of martyrs were considered sacred and served as the first relics, and their resting places became shrines. Many Christians desired to be buried alongside known martyrs, leading to a funerary real estate boom. The Christian Church, for its part, actively participated in the veneration of martyrs. Accounts of the deaths of martyrs were documented and carefully preserved for future generations. Many of these stories have qualities that suggest their primary goal was instruction, so that people might follow the example of the martyrs, rather than simply recording events. Many accounts feature passages in which the condemned Christian's words spoken to his or her persecutor are directly quoted as if they are transcriptions, such as those spoken by the martyr Speratus to his persecutor, Saturnius: "I do not recognize the empire of this world; but rather I serve that God, whom no man has seen nor can see. I have not stolen, but if I buy anything, I pay the tax, because I recognize my Lord, the King of Kings and Emperor to all peoples."

Many of these exchanges cannot be verified, taking place in private or spoken in a crowded arena with thousands of screaming spectators, and so they are likely fictionalized. However, a fair number have been verified by historians to be authentic. These transcend the politicized statements used by the early Christian Church to highlight the faithful's piety to capture the reality of persecution: ordinary people steadfastly enduring extraordinary suffering.

## St. Perpetua

The persecutions between the first and third centuries CE minted a number of saints, many of whose stories were documented by the Christian Church. Known as **passions**, these accounts were meant to serve as instructional manuals to other Christians whose faith was tested. Among these is a fascinating journal written by a female martyr in North Africa named Perpetua. Perpetua's account is on its own historically

PAR LOUIS LASSALLE

**St. Perpetua's firsthand account of her imprisonment offers a valuable insight into the experience of the early Christian martyrs. Perpetua is standing.**

significant because it is an exceptional piece of writing in Latin by an ancient female author, but it is also a testament to both the certainty of a Christian's faith in the face of adversity as well as the individuality and independence of a woman.

The prologue to Perpetua's account notes that she was born into nobility, benefitted from liberal education, married well, and had a son by the time she was twenty-two. However, Perpetua converted to Christianity, which drove a wedge between her and her family, particularly her father, who commanded her to abandon her faith. Perpetua recounts one such argument with her father:

> "Father," I said, "for the sake of argument, do you see this vase, or whatever you want to call it, lying here?"
>
> And he said, "Yes, I see it."
>
> And I said to him, "Can you call it by any other name than what it is?"
>
> And he said, "No, you can't."
>
> "So," I said, "I cannot call myself anything other than what I am—a Christian."
>
> Merely hearing this word upset my father greatly. He threw himself at me with such violence that it seemed he wanted to tear my eyes out.

The issue of faith over family would force Perpetua to make an even more difficult choice: between martyrdom and motherhood. Perpetua was taken into custody by the authorities and held in prison until such time that she gave up her religion or was executed. At first, Perpetua brought her suckling child into prison with her, but she realized that the boy was suffering from malnourishment. Had she recanted, she would have been allowed to leave with her child; instead, Perpetua gave her son to her mother and brother to care for. Perpetua's account says that the boy was given back to her once he had regained some health but that she again handed him to her family once he started to starve again. At last, Perpetua was told in her cell that the boy would not take to her again. Thus, her own child seemed to abandon her.

Perpetua's firsthand accounts end the day before her execution in 204 in the Carthage arena, but supplementary epilogues describe her fate. Prior to entering the arena, the guards tried to force Perpetua and the other martyrs to dress in robes honoring the Roman gods. Perpetua refused, saying "For this cause came we willingly unto this, that our liberty might not be obscured. For this cause have we devoted our lives, that we might do no such thing as this; this we agreed with you." Instead, the guards stripped the women naked, but the crowd reacted negatively to this, so Perpetua was again clothed. The male martyrs were thrown to a leopard and a bear, and Perpetua and the other female martyr, known as Felicity, were attacked by a heifer. Perpetua apparently fell into an unconscious state, what the account calls a "religious ecstasy," and did not realize that she was mauled nearly to death by the cow. At last, the martyrs were lined up and their throats cut.

## The Pattern of Persecution

The emperors who followed Nero had an inconsistent record in rooting out Christianity. More often than not, persecuting Christians served as a political diversion for emperors struggling to maintain control. Other times, persecutions that lacked imperial administrative organization were matters of personal agendas by governors who had grown frustrated by the activity of the religious radicals in their provinces. Periods of persecution that had started with intensity usually fizzled out as arbitrarily as they had started.

An example of this waxing and waning of interest in eradicating Christianity comes from Pliny the Younger, a government official and historian. (Pliny's eyewitness account of the eruption of Mount Vesuvius serves as the basis for much of what historians know about the destruction of Pompeii.) Around 112 CE, Pliny was appointed by the emperor Trajan to assist with the administration of the province of Bithynia in Asia Minor. While in the city of either Amisus or Amastris, an anonymous group of citizens approached Pliny to complain about Christians living in the area. It is unclear what the complaint was exactly, but it seems that many of the citizens were butchers and merchants whose business was poor. The Christians were refusing to purchase and eat meat that had come from animals slaughtered in pagan sacrifices, a boycott called for by Paul decades earlier. This disrupted trade in the area. Evidence for this theory comes from the conclusion of a letter Pliny had written in which he says, "Flesh of sacrificial victims is on sale everywhere, though up till recently scarcely anyone could be found to buy it."

As accomplished an administrator as he was, Pliny didn't know what to make of Christianity in general:

I have never been present at an examination of Christians. Consequently, I do not know the nature of the extent of the punishments usually meted out to them, nor the grounds for starting an investigation and how far it should be pressed. Nor am I at all sure … whether it is the mere name of Christian which is punishable, even if innocent of crime, or rather crimes associated with the name.

Pliny collected a number of these Christians who had been anonymously identified to him. He interrogated and tortured those who seemed as if they were leading the community, but Pliny found that the common accusations of Christian wantonness and debauchery were unfounded.

They declared that the sum total of their guilt or error amounted to no more than this; they had met regularly before dawn on a fixed day to chant verses alternately among themselves in honor of Christ as if to a god, and also to bind themselves by oath, not for any criminal purpose, but to abstain from theft, robbery, and adultery, to commit no breach of trust and not to deny a despot when called upon to restore it. After this ceremony it had been their custom to disperse and reassemble later to take food of an ordinary harmless kind.

Unsure of what to do, Pliny wrote to Trajan, who was as thoughtful as Nero was megalomaniacal, for advice. Trajan's response was simply to ignore anonymous complaints about others, calling them "a very bad example and unworthy of our time."

Despite Trajan's vague response, Pliny sent some of the Christians he had interrogated to be executed. Though doubtful that a person should be punished simply for being Christian, Pliny believed it was sufficient that they were pigheaded about their beliefs, no less in front of a Roman official: "Whatever the nature of their admission, I am convinced that their stubbornness and unshakeable obstinacy ought not go unpunished."

Trajan himself did not order the persecution of Christians on anything close to the scale of predecessors such as Domitian, but he did order the execution of Ignatius, the **Bishop** of Antioch, and of Simeon, the Bishop of Jerusalem.

## Crisis of Empire

The third century saw the Roman Empire in crisis. Rome reached its greatest extent under the Emperor Trajan, but after he died in 117, the empire ceased to expand as civilizations on its frontier started to push back against encroachment. Up to this point, the Romans funded their incessant expansion through the wealth collected from newly conquered lands; now, Rome fought constant wars on the frontier without expanding its pool of taxable territories. Keeping the army well paid and happy became the first priority—if soldiers began to defect en masse, there would be nothing to prevent the barbarians from sweeping down through the empire. The emperors were forced to raise taxes to extraordinary levels, which few people could afford. Many lower-class Romans in turn left their homes and resorted to supporting themselves through crime such as highway robbery. The need for policing within the empire grew, which meant more resources were

# The Catacombs

The early Christians left a mysterious relic from their time in Rome, a complex network of subterranean tunnels spanning over 68 square miles (176 square kilometers) known as the **catacombs**. The catacombs got their name from *In catacumbas*, a particular underground passage situated along the Appian Way, ancient Rome's major thoroughfare. Knowledge of the locations of the catacombs survived past the early Christian period.

Contrary to popular belief, the catacombs were not hideouts for Christians seeking to escape the scrutiny of their persecutors. Historians believe that rumor was started by Catholics during the Counter-Reformation of the mid-sixteenth century, when religious separatists known generally as Protestants were questioning the

The Catacombs of Priscilla, pictured above, is one of a number of subterranean networks used by early Christians to bury their dead.

piety of the Catholic Church, which is headquartered in Rome. Roman government records suggest that Christian communities were acquiring land-use permits to construct tunnels for burial purposes near the end of the second century. Not only did the Romans know about the location and general scope of the catacombs, they approved them with a rubber stamp.

Instead, the catacombs were simply cemeteries, places for quiet and dignified burials. The Christian catacombs were modeled after similar Jewish catacombs in Rome, which date back to the first century. Between the second and ninth centuries, Christians from around Rome buried hundreds of thousands of their dead in the catacombs. Archaeologists estimate that the catacombs house 875,000 bodies, though there remain many unexplored corners of the catacombs, and it is thought that many catacombs haven't even been discovered.

diverted to the army and led to even greater levels of taxation and greater crime.

Complicating matters in the western part of the empire was an influx of warlike tribes from central Asia. This migration had been going on for centuries, and European tribes were, in turn, forced to migrate west and south into Roman-controlled lands. In the winter of 166–167, the Danube River, located in central Europe, froze, allowing thousands of barbarian invaders to cross and ransack the empire's northern territories.

Meanwhile, the eastern half of the empire was threatened by the rise of a new kingdom in Iran called the Sassanids, who had won independence from the Parthians. With their newfound autonomy, the Sassanids resolved to take revenge on the West, which had forced its culture on Iran since the time of Alexander the Great. In 260, the Sassanid prince Shapur fought an army of Roman soldiers under the emperor Valerian. The Sassanids captured Valerian, who later died as Shapur's prisoner, to the embarrassment and horror of the empire.

At home, Rome suffered from a succession of emperors who were inept, delusional, and psychotic—sometimes a combination of the three. Although the Flavian and Antonine dynasties of the first and second centuries featured a number of capable rulers, the last of the Antonines, Commodus, fell more in line with the likes of Nero. Commodus was murdered by his mistress Marcia (interestingly the first Christian to come to prominence in the imperial court), who feared Commodus would murder her. The civil war that followed came to an end when an army officer named Septimus Severus assumed the throne. Severus's heirs proved to be brutal rulers and were summarily assassinated. Between Severus's death in 211 and the emperor Diocletian's ascendence in 284, only a handful of emperors died from natural causes—the rest were murdered.

With everything seeming to fall apart both abroad and at home, many people turned toward religion for comfort in the hope of better days to come. A few found renewed enthusiasm for the Roman gods of old, but many others—both ordinary people and aristocrats alike—explored Christianity, which offered a sense of oneness and community in the place of paranoia, rules in the place of chaos, and purity in the place of unwholesomeness. By the end of the second century, Christianity had grown large enough to have a presence in the highest echelons in Roman society, including the imperial palace itself.

Many Romans with traditionalist attitudes, however, grew concerned about this rise. Throughout the second century, there arose a number of concentrated imperial efforts to identify and prosecute Christians. In 202, Septimus Severus issued an edict that forbade people from converting to either Christianity or Judaism. Severus's edict gave support to several small-scale persecutions during his reign as well as the reigns of his sons. Meanwhile, intellectuals began writing against Christianity, which, with all its talk of openness to all and a new spiritual law, they believed was a foreign conspiracy to subvert the empire from within. Among these traditionalist writers was Celsus, who believed the old gods of Rome were the pillars of the empire, and that the worship of a dead carpenter from Judaea was idiotic. Should Rome give way to Christianity, Celsus wrote, "earthly things would come into the power of the most lawless and savage barbarians."

The emperor Decius, who seized power in 249, agreed with Celsus's evaluation. He believed that Rome's troubles were punishment from the ancient gods, who had grown angry with the Romans for declining to offer sacrifices. Decius endeavored to enforce an unprecedented traditionalist policy in which sacrifice was ordered for every household in the empire and prosecution awaited those who would not obey. The group that had most obviously refused to make sacrifices was the Christians. Under Decius's law, those who performed sacrifices would be issued a certificate proving they had done so; those who were found without such a certificate would be subjected to imprisonment and occasionally death.

What Decius's persecution lacked in brutality like Nero's it made up for with administrative efficiency. Soon after the policy was enacted in 250, practically every Christian throughout the empire was identified and harassed. Decius's policy was revived again by two later emperors and did not end until 260, when Emperor Gallienus believed that Rome's time, attention, and resources would be better spent on more pressing foreign threats.

Although only a handful of Christians died as a result of Decius's policy, it nevertheless dealt a massive blow to the Christian Church's morale. Counter to the example set by the martyrs of the first century, most Christians at this time actually abandoned the religion. Church leaders known as bishops who defiantly abided by their faith fell victim to execution and were no longer around, and those who fled or went into hiding were criticized by those who suffered for their faith. Meanwhile, many ordinary Christians, bereft of their most fervent leaders and abandoned by those who survived, decided it was better to simply obey rather than defy the emperor. As troubling as this crisis was, however, Christianity had yet to face its greatest and most ruthless threat.

## Diocletian and the Great Persecution

The political turmoil that had been troubling the empire for nearly a century came to an end when Gaius Aurelius Valerius Diocletianus, known simply as Diocletian, seized control in

284. Before the end of his reign, when he abdicated power in May 305, the ambitious Diocletian embarked on a series of unprecedented reforms that would forever alter the shape of the empire. Among these reforms was a program designed to completely wipe Christianity from the face of the earth.

Diocletian was born to humble circumstances in 245 in the province of Dalmatia, located in the Balkans in the northeast of the empire. His father was a scribe to a senator, though it seems he was at one point a slave. Diocletian joined the army and quickly rose to prominence among the ranks. Eventually, the emperor Carinus appointed Diocletian an army chief in a campaign against the Persians. During the campaign, Carinus's brother and co-emperor Numerian, who had been traveling with the army, was found dead. Most suspected that Numerian's adoptive father, a prefect in the Praetorian Guard, was responsible. The army declared Diocletian emperor, and Diocletian arrested Aper, declared him guilty of murder, and executed him before the troops. Diocletian had years before received a prophecy that he would become emperor after he killed a boar, which in Latin is *aper*; thus, Diocletian seized the opportunity to kill Aper, believing it to fulfill his destiny. In reality, Numerian most likely died an unexpected but natural death.

Diocletian held power only in the lands his army occupied in Asia Minor and Syria; the rest of the empire continued to follow Carinus. Diocletian was not Carinus's only concern, as another army commander had also started a revolt in the north of Italy. Once Carinus killed his other rival, he turned his attention to Diocletian. Their two armies met near

# Periods of Persecution

**53 CE:** Emperor Claudius (reigned 41–54) orders the expulsion of Jews, including Christians, who were then considered by the government to be a sect within Judaism, from the city of Rome for disturbing the peace.

**64 CE:** In the wake of a fire that destroyed most of Rome, Emperor Nero (reigned 54–68) begins the first focused persecution of Christians as a way to distract the public from its negative opinion of him.

**81 CE:** After Emperor Domitian (reigned 81–96) becomes the first Roman emperor to deify himself during his lifetime, he embarks on a policy of persecution of those who will not recognize his divinity, including Jews, in particular, as well as Christians.

**111–113 CE:** In correspondence with Pliny, the administrator of the province of Bithynia, Emperor Trajan (reigned 98–117) establishes a sort of code for meting out punishment to Christians. According to these letters, investigations into Christians, including those prompted by complaints, are not permissible, but those who admit to being Christian deserve death, while those who make the accepted sacrifices may be released.

**Circa mid-second century CE:** Although no official imperial edicts against Christians dating from the reign of Marcus Aurelius (reigned 161–180) have been discovered, localized persecution of Christians in Rome's provinces flourished, as did writings by such intellectuals as Celsus, who condemned Christian theology.

**Circa 202–203 CE:** Persecutions again break out under Emperor Septimus Severus (reigned 193–211), especially in Syria and North Africa, where St. Perpetua is martyred. In 202, Septimus Severus issues an edict declaring it illegal to convert to either Judaism or Christianity.

**249–251 CE:** The first concentrated, empire-wide persecution of Christians accompanies the reign of Emperor Decius, who believed that the threats to the empire of the third century owed to the fact that traditional Roman religion was neglected. Administrators throughout the empire identify Christians due to their lack of documentation certifying that the holder had made the mandated sacrifices.

**Circa 257–259 CE:** The Emperor Valerian (reigned 253–260) officially revokes certain rights allowed to Christians by earlier emperors, including the right to assemble and enter the catacombs, and proceeds to issue edicts designed to harass Christians, including a command exiling all clergy, the proscription of death for Christian leaders, and threats of property confiscation and exile for aristocratic Christians.

**303–313:** The Great Persecution, begun under Emperor Diocletian (reigned 284–305), is concentrated largely in the eastern half of the Empire and is characterized by the destruction of Christian churches and sacred texts, the loss of rights for Christians, the imprisonment of Christian leaders, and forced sacrifice, refusal of which is punished by execution. The persecution persists in pockets of the empire until 313, when Emperor Constantine (reigned 306–337) orders the toleration of Christians with the Edict of Milan.

present-day Belgrade, Serbia. Diocletian would likely have lost, but Carinus was assassinated by a group of soldiers. By the summer of 285, Diocletian was the last proclaimed emperor left standing.

Diocletian recognized the problems that plagued the empire. These included the threat of foreign invasion, the frequency of civil wars and revolts instigated by rogue military commanders, and the size of the empire, which made efficient administration impossible. After all, Diocletian's own rise to power was helped by the chaos these issues created. Shortly after consolidating his power, he made a move that surprised many. In 286, he divided control of the empire between himself and a former companion whom Diocletian trusted, a fellow soldier from a humble background named Maximian, in order to streamline the administration of the empire. Although the official capital of the empire remained Rome, and the empire itself was theoretically whole, it now had two centers of command. Diocletian installed Maximian in Milan, in the north of Italy, to keep an eye on the west, and he situated himself in Nicomedia, near the eastern frontier.

Diocletian's reform was successful. With two capable heads concentrating on one of two halves, the empire was able to repel the constant invasions as well as quell uprisings within its borders. Eventually, the administration of the empire was further divided, as both Diocletian and Maximian chose their own trusted overseers to tend to large swaths within their own territories. This arrangement came to be known as the "tetrarchy," the "rule of four." Diocletian's division laid the groundwork for the official split between the Western and Eastern Roman Empires and the rise of the Byzantine Empire.

Diocletian believed that both his prophesied rise to power as well as the success with which he brought control to the empire indicated that his rule was ordained by the gods. He believed that his rise to power was orchestrated by the gods so that he might rekindle interest in the ancient cults

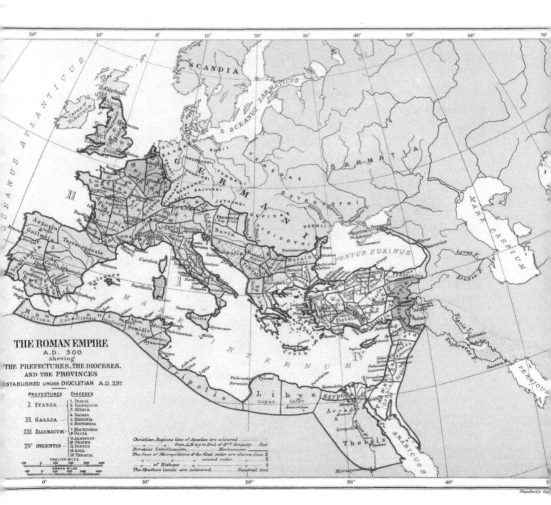

This map illustrates the size of the Roman Empire under Diocletian.

and keep the honor of the gods alive among humanity. He considered Maximian and himself to be "sons of gods and creators of gods" and took to calling himself Jovius (Jove or Jupiter, the king of the Roman gods) and Maximian Heculius (Hercules). Soon, coins and inscriptions included the epithet "*dominus et deus*" ("Lord and God") after Diocletian's name.

As time wore on, Diocletian's religious conservatism sparked deeper and deeper mistrust of new religions, particularly Christianity. In 302, Diocletian officially declared, "The ancient religion ought not to be censured by a new one. For it is the height of criminality to reverse that which the ancestors had defined, once and for all, things which hold and preserve their recognized place and course." To Diocletian, the reason for the recent chaos in the empire was simple: the ancient Roman gods had grown angry with the Romans, who had permitted new "heathen" religions to grow within their borders while neglecting to make the sacrifices that had been performed for centuries. Therefore, Diocletian was led to believe that the success of the empire hinged on strict adherence to traditional religion and the eradication of corrupting religious influences from the likes of Christianity.

Diocletian's reign was generally characterized as an administrative success, stemming the empire's decline through a savvy division of power, but the last years of his rule were darkened by the most severe state-sponsored bout of persecution directed at Christians the empire had yet seen. In the 290s, a group of military officers, including Galerius, the additional overseer Diocletian had chosen for his eastern territories, increasingly fed into Diocletian's traditionalist attitudes. They suggested that Diocletian follow his inclinations to root out those groups that would not honor the gods and thereby protect the empire through sacrifice. In 303, Diocletian launched a concentrated assault on all sources of Christian influence: churches, sacred texts, and especially bishops and other members of the clergy. Persecution was not so intense in the West, where Maximian's colleague Constantius harbored some sympathy for Christians, but suppression of Christians raged in many eastern parts of the empire for eleven years. During this time, Christian Church leaders were rounded up and ordered to make sacrifices to the pagan gods. Those who refused were executed, including the bishop of Nicomedia, the leader of the Christian community within Diocletian's own eastern headquarters, who was beheaded. According to historian Diarmaid MacCulloch, nearly half of recorded martyrdoms in Christianity's early history—between 3,000 and 3,500 Christians—date to this period, which became known as "The Great Persecution."

Fortunately for the Christian Church, this decade-long attack on Christianity would be the tenth and last it would suffer under the Romans. As it had done before, the Christian Church weathered the Great Persecution. Soon after Diocletian's abdication, a new emperor rose to power, one who would not only halt the centuries-long cycle in which periods of peace were followed by periods of official suppression of Christians, but who would actively work to legitimize the religion within the empire and even convert himself, forever changing the course of history.

# FOUR

# Defending the Faith

The mission to adjust mainstream Roman perspectives on Christianity persisted throughout Christianity's spread. Although the martyrs made emotional appeals during periods of persecution, they were not the only defenders of the faith. Christianity was a movement that transcended borders, class, and race, and believers from all walks of life used the skills at their disposal to combat prejudice.

Among the earliest defenders of Christians were intellectuals who had benefitted from rigorous philosophical education. These writers penned a number of works, known as **apologies**, which tried to dispel the rumors about Christian beliefs and rituals that in part fueled persecution. An apology in this sense, unlike the more common understanding as a regretful acknowledgment of an offense, comes from the Greek word *apologia*, meaning to "speak in return," and is inspired by the discourses of ancient Greek philosophers such as Socrates, Plato, and Aristotle. An apology is a reasoned

*Opposite: St. Lawrence Feeding the Poor* was painted by Fra Angelico. St. Lawrence was among the many Christians who took to defending their faith in front of the Romans, and he was later burned to death.

argument written to justify a particular belief. Occasionally, these writings would also criticize the prevailing culture, in a form known as the **polemic**. Although many of the rituals of Christianity, such as communion and baptism, had been well established from early on, Christianity's theology was still in its early stages of development. With the help of these thinkers, known as apologists, and their logical defenses, Christianity's tradition of intellectual discourse would expand greatly despite these periods of persecution; however, this explosion of discussion combined with the isolation of many Christian communities contributed to the development of rival factions preaching conflicting dogmas within Christianity as a whole.

## St. Justin Martyr

One of the earliest Christian apologists was Justin Martyr. Of the many fathers of the Christian Church from the second century CE, Justin's biography is most complete, thanks to a number of well-preserved documents written by Justin in which he reveals personal information about his studies and conversion. Justin was born around 100 CE into a pagan family of Greek origin in a predominantly Jewish community of Flavia Neapolis, located in the modern-day West Bank, Palestine. Justin was educated in Greek philosophy, especially in Platonic philosophy. In one of his works, *Dialogue with the Jew Tryphon*, Justin mentions how his studies in Platonism inclined him toward Christianity. He writes that he once had a discussion with a mysterious man who, taking Justin's belief that God was perfect and unchanging, reasoned that imperfect and changeable humans could not come to know God on their own but needed the guidance of prophets who had been inspired by God to know him.

Some time around 130 CE, Justin writes in his *Second Apology* that he encountered the scene of Christians being martyred: "When I was a disciple of Plato, hearing the accusations made against the Christians and seeing them intrepid in the face of death and of all that men fear, I said to myself that it was impossible that they should be living in evil and in the love of pleasure." From then on, Justin was moved by the martyrs' moral strength. He converted and went on to write a number of defenses of his new religion, explaining that Christianity did not threaten the empire's political or moral foundations. In several of his works, Justin

This mosaic from the Mount of the Beatitudes shows Justin Martyr's beheading.

draws parallels between concepts in Greek philosophy and those in Christianity, such as the duality of spiritual and physical existence ruled by a perfect and preexistent being, as well as the idea that time is marching inexorably to a conclusion of the physical world. However, perhaps above these intellectual discussions, Justin takes particular notice of the piety of Christians and their capacity to endure extraordinary pain in service of their conviction.

In his *Second Apology*, Justin writes that he expects to be targeted for persecution himself, and around 165 CE, Justin's prediction came to fruition: the prefect Rusticus rounded up Justin and six of his companions and commanded them to make sacrifices to the Roman gods. Echoing so many other martyrs before him, Justin refused, saying that he would make himself impure when he was already pure and willingly welcomed the tortures that awaited his refusal. Justin and his companions were whipped and eventually beheaded, but not before praying to God and Jesus Christ.

## Origen of Alexandria

Among the most influential Christian apologists was Origen of Alexandria. Origen was born in 185 CE in Alexandria, Egypt, and came of age during Septimus Severus's persecution. According to the Christian historian Eusebius, Origen's family was prominent in the Christian community, and his father was himself martyred. Origen's family was determined to provide a top-notch education for their son, who was instructed both in biblical studies as well as traditional Hellenistic subjects, including mathematics, philosophy, and rhetoric. Origen

Origen's use of pagan philosophers to defend Christianity tried to legitimize the religion to its persecutors.

proved a brilliant scholar, amassing a large library of philosophical texts and even taking over as headmaster of the Christian school in Alexandria at the age of seventeen.

Like Paul of Tarsus, Origen's success as a leader in the early Christian Church benefitted from a broad education that covered his own monotheistic beliefs as well as the ideas of pagan intellectuals, especially Plato and the stoic philosophers. Origen was a prolific writer, penning by some estimates six thousand letters, homilies, treatises, and biblical commentaries. This thrust him into the turbulent waters of Christian theology, earned him a reputation as a thoughtful speaker throughout the empire, and eventually led to a school of thought known as Origenism. Among Origen's writings was the treatise *De principiis* (*On the Principles*, ca. 230), which explained what qualifies a Christian as truly faithful. These core principles included belief in the tripartite, preexisting God or Holy Trinity—God the Creator, Jesus as God made flesh, and the Holy Spirit—the free will of rational human beings; the existence of souls outside of the body; and the impermanence of the physical world, which is to be concluded by a final judgment.

In addition to setting down his vision of Christian doctrine, Origen also used his talents in writing and philosophy to defend Christianity from pagan attacks. In 248, Origen wrote *Contra Celsum* (*Against Celsus*), an influential apology directed at the criticisms of Christianity by a traditionalist intellectual named Celsus. In the second century, Celsus wrote *Alethes logos* (*The True Doctrine*), which argued that Christianity was a religion for simpletons born in the cultural backwaters of Palestine. To Celsus, Christians used the faith as a philosophical presupposition, which clouded their thinking and was therefore bad philosophy. The proliferation of Christian belief therefore threatened the sophistication and purity of developed classical culture. Celsus's attack proved popular among the pagan intelligentsia of the second century, which made it an ideal target for Origen. In *Contra Celsum*, Origen used the same Platonic ideals Celsus himself used, arguing that a true philosopher could reasonably use Christianity as a framework for viewing the world like any other. By using the same works that served as the foundation for pagan Greco-Roman culture to support Christian culture, Origen managed to demonstrate to his readers that Christianity was not only nonthreatening to the empire but shared a similar intellectual heritage that made it deserving of respect.

Origen's influence in the development of Christianity is great. His expositions of the Gospels were widely used (and plagiarized) by later Christian writers, and his beliefs are commonly thought to have contributed to the rise of monasticism. According to St. Jerome, a Christian writer celebrated for translating the Bible into Latin, Origen's legacy in the early Christian Church is second only to the apostles. However, Origen's reliance on pagan philosophy has also lead many to accuse him of heresy. Some scholars believed Origen to have said Jesus was subordinate to God the Father in the Holy Trinity, contrary to orthodox Christian belief, which places them as equals. The belief likely led to the development of a troubling heresy known as **Arianism**, which rose to prominence in Origen's hometown of Alexandria (see chapter 5). Later adherents of Origenism also caused a stir with their belief in the preexistence of souls and universal salvation, which prompted the Emperor Justinian I to denounce Origen in the mid-sixth century.

There were dozens more apologists in addition to St. Justin Martyr and Origen of Alexandria throughout the centuries as Christianity spread throughout the Roman Empire. For all the work the apologists did in their attempts to legitimize Christianity's morality and theology within the Roman Empire, they could do little to stop the root causes for persecution, which generally involved periods when emperors and other regional rulers used public spectacles of Christian martyrs to distract the masses. Many apologists, like Justin Martyr,

# St. Maximilian of Theveste

The transcendental nature of Christianity meant that it impacted all corners of life in the Roman Empire, from the everyday and private to the political and public. Christianity's influence was felt even in the most iconic and storied of ancient Roman institutions: the military. Many soldiers converted to Christianity, including an officer known as Cornelius, who, according to legend, was the first Gentile to convert to Christianity.

The experience of soldiers who converted often reflected the ebb and flow of persecutions, as well as the intellectual debate going on within Christianity itself, particularly the morality of war. Christians have historically supported a moderate position toward certain types of violence, such as self-defense and "just war," which has been explained by eminent Christian theologians such as St. Augustine and St. Thomas Aquinas. However, many early Christians, such as the apologist Tertullian, believed that Jesus preached a radical pacifism that prohibited violence of any kind.

Among those Christians who maintained this belief was a man named Maximilian of Theveste, modern-day Tébessa, Algeria. In the late third century CE, imperial agents were recruiting soldiers for the army stationed in North Africa. Because Maximilian's father was a soldier, he was required to serve also. When the recruiters approached him, Maximilian refused, saying that he could not serve because he was a Christian, arguing that wearing the uniform, which included a necklace emblazoned with the emperor's image, was idolatry and that to fight was a sin. When the recruiters threatened him with execution, he said, "I will not die; even if I do depart the world, my spirit will live with my Lord Christ."

Maximilian was sentenced to die by the sword in 296, a fate which he went to happily. He was later made a saint in the Catholic Church, which celebrates his feast day (the day a saint is remembered with a special mention, a scripture reading, and prayers) on March 12.

were officially suppressed and forced to make their deaths into emotional testaments to the strength of their personal conviction that Jesus was the savior of mankind.

The apologists contributed to the intellectual development of Christianity and worked to lend credibility to the Eastern religion by incorporating and synthesizing philosophical arguments from Western sources. Arguably the most common of these ancient pagan sources was Plato, whose ideas were used by both Justin Martyr and Origen. Platonic parallels with Christianity were numerous, including Plato's general understanding of God as perfect and unchangeable and the notion that physical existence is a fundamentally imperfect alteration of deeper spiritual truth. Because of this, Plato's philosophy became a major source of information for later Christian theologians, who sought to connect Christianity to those theories while proving that it logically perfects them.

While the overarching goal of the apologists was to defend their faith against the rampant speculation of outsiders which was used as justification for persecution, the work of many apologists had the unintended consequences of sowing dissension within the Christian Church. Reliance on ancient pagan scholars helped to establish Christianity's philosophical heritage on the one hand, but on the other it caused many Christians to suspect that certain apologists were perverting the monotheistic faith with pagan ideas. Additionally, the isolation of many of the apologists, coupled with the fact that Christian orthodoxy (right doctrine) and orthopraxy (right practice) were still being settled, contributed to the fracturing of the global Christian Church. This situation changed once Constantine made Christianity legal. That allowed the Christian Church to effectively unify in one ecclesiastical jurisdiction. It began the task of combatting contradictory theologies, many of which had roots in the writings of apologists.

Christian apologists frequently drew on the writings of Plato (*seated*) to support their arguments.

# FIVE

# Constantine and the New Christian Empire

On October 29, 312 CE, Flavius Valerius Constantinus, known simply as Constantine, marched into Rome. Fresh from a victory in a civil war with his rival to the throne, Constantine now commanded all the powers of the Roman Empire. However, rather than stop at the altars where his predecessors had for centuries made sacrifices to the ancient gods during their triumphant marches into the city, Constantine made his way directly to the palace. Unlike those other emperors, Constantine had had an unusual vision of the Christian God just days before the victory that secured his rule. As with the Jewish conquests millennia ago, as with Jesus's resurrection and triumph over death, it seems God's hand had once again manipulated world events, and Constantine's rule would prove a pioneering one.

*Opposite: The Vision of Constantine from the French school in the nineteenth century.*

# Constantine's Rise to Power

Constantine was born in modern-day Serbia sometime in the late 280s CE, the only son of an army officer named Flavius Valerius Constantius, known simply as Constantius. In 293, Constantius was appointed deputy emperor in the West as a member of Diocletian's tetrarchy. He was given the name Constantius I Chlorus and was sent to serve under Maximian in the western part of the empire while his son Constantine lived in Diocletian's palace at Nicomedia in the East. Constantine grew up in Diocletian's shadow and was present in the imperial court during the Great Persecution.

The stability Diocletian's reign had brought to the empire quickly eroded when he, along with Maximian, abdicated the throne. Constantius was installed in Maximian's position in the West, but his son Constantine was passed over for rule when Constantius was replaced by Flavius Valerius Severus. In the early 300s, Constantine joined his father in the campaign in Britannia (Britain). When Constantius died at Eboracum (modern-day York) in 306, the armies under his command declared Constantine the new emperor.

From there, Constantine joined the number of civil wars raging throughout the empire. Maximian's son Maxentius, like Constantine, believed he deserved to inherit rule of his father's corner of the empire. With his father's help, Maxentius rebelled against Severus from Rome and overthrew him. When Maxentius rejected his father just after their victory, Maximian joined Constantine's forces in the North. However, while Constantine was battling in Gaul (modern-day France),

This statue of Constantine is located in York, England, at the site where his armies declared him emperor.

Maximian declared that Constantine had died and that he was the new emperor. Constantine hunted his betrayer down, and Maximian committed suicide.

By this point, Maxentius was the last rival standing in Constantine's way. Around the time of his father's death, Maxentius's popularity had started to wane owing to an increase in taxes to fund the emperor's personal vanity projects, including a statue of himself. Shortly after riots broke out in the capital, Constantine assembled tens of thousands of troops and crossed the Alps into Italy. Constantine and Maxentius met at the Milvian Bridge outside Rome in the fall of 312 CE. Although outnumbered, Constantine's army crushed Maxentius's forces. With Maxentius removed, Constantine marched into Rome as emperor.

## Constantine's Conversion

At some point before the Battle of Milvian Bridge, Constantine saw something that would change not only power in Rome but the power of Christianity in the West. Accounts of what exactly Constantine saw differ. Most of what is believed to have happened comes from two Christian writers, Lactantius and Eusebius. Lactantius writes that Jesus Christ appeared to Constantine the night before the battle in a dream, in which he instructed Constantine to paint the Christian symbol Chi-Rho on his soldiers' shields. Eusebius's account, however, was related to him by Constantine himself late in the emperor's life. According to Eusebius, Constantine looked into the sky the day before the battle and saw the image of a cross superimposed over the sun. Below it was written, *"In hoc signo, vinces"* — "In this sign, conquer." The following day, he had his soldiers paint the Christian symbol onto their shields.

Also known as the labarum, the Chi-Rho Constantine had ordered his troops to paint on their shields consists of an X (chi) and a P (rho) overlaid one another. The word "Chi-Rho" derives from the first two Greek letters for "Christ." Apparently, the symbol is of Constantine's design, as it has no precedent in either scripture or early Christian symbology; however, with Constantine's rise to power, it would become known the world over. Not only did Constantine continue the practice of having the Chi-Rho appear on shields, but it also became the official standard for Rome's armies and was printed on small change currency circulating throughout the empire.

While it is unclear what precipitated Constantine's conversion, the fact remains that Constantine had an experience that inclined him toward Christianity. After the battle, Constantine made it known that he believed he owed his success at Milvian Bridge to the Christian God. Well into his rule, he wrote that all of his successes were due to that God alone, and later, he wrote to Shapur II, the young king of Persia, "Him [Jesus Christ] I call upon with bended knee, shunning all abominable blood and hateful odors [of pagan sacrifice]."

Constantine was not baptized until he was on his deathbed in 337; however, he personally adopted the religion and publicly strove to permanently establish it within the Roman Empire. A year after Constantine's victory over Maxentius, he and the eastern emperor, Licinius (Constantine's temporary ally), together issued the Edict of Milan, which guaranteed Christians rights equal to those of any other cult throughout the empire. At the time, there were still several emperors vying for control in the East in addition to Licinius, and many of these were continuing to persecute Christians as Diocletian had done. Constantine led a campaign against these pretenders, in part to ensure his decree was carried out but primarily to remove any threats to his power. As he collected more victories, he commanded his soldiers to say a prayer in thanks to the Christian God.

Eventually, Constantine's alliance with Licinius weakened to the point that the two battled for control of the empire. Because Constantine was pro-Christian, Licinius turned against the Christians in his realm in order to erode his rival's base of support in the East. Constantine became the sole emperor after Licinius was murdered in 324. With him died the last threat of violence directed at Christians in the Roman Empire.

# A "Roman" Conversion

On the surface, it may seem like Diocletian and Constantine were fundamentally different emperors; after all, one had instituted a policy of persecution of Christians so broad and devastating that it became known as "The Great Persecution," while the other converted to Christianity and made it the religion of the realm, earning him the nickname "Constantine the Great." However, Constantine and Diocletian were not very different from one another. Both were accomplished military commanders with imperial ambitions, and both had found opportunity to advance their own power in the chaos resulting from civil wars. However, the most fascinating quality they share is the ways in which religion affected the circumstances of their rule.

Both Diocletian and Constantine believed that their rise to power was preordained by divine powers. Both emperors believed that the observance of *religio,* that is, "correct religion," corresponded to the success of the empire. For Diocletian, *religio* was the faith of his ancient Roman forefathers. Diocletian sought to preserve the Roman Empire as it had been known for centuries by enacting policies to maintain the ancient ways. Meanwhile, Constantine's vision before the Battle of Milvian Bridge inspired him to believe that the God of Christianity would guarantee both personal power and prosperity for the empire—a new religion for a new Rome. For both Diocletian and Constantine, their faith in their respective religions seems to have been genuinely felt, but their apparent piety was a means to the end of political success.

# Imperial Christianity

By this time, Christianity was hardly a small group of pious believers from the dregs of society, constantly beleaguered by the pagan establishment—the ease with which Emperor Constantine personally adopted and established Christianity within a decade of Diocletian's persecution is proof alone. While the exact number of Christians at this time is impossible to gather, historian Peter Brown estimates that as much as 10 percent of the Roman Empire's population identified as Christian, with the majority collecting in Asia Minor, Syria, and major population centers around the Mediterranean. Furthermore, Christians could be found in the highest strata of Roman society well before Constantine's conversion. The fact is that Christianity was a large religion whose adherents were as multifaceted as the Roman Empire itself. Some Christians were poor while some were wealthy; some were slaves and some owned slaves; some were disenfranchised while some wielded ultimate power.

Christianity, aided by the emperor's adoption of its principles, was granted institutional legitimacy practically overnight, and Constantine worked to integrate Christianity into mainstream Roman culture. He proclaimed that Christianity would share the same respect as the official pagan cults. The emperor welcomed Christian clergy into his court. He showered wealth and gifts on the Christian Church, including monuments in honor of the God of Christianity, magnificent architectural projects, and fifty exquisitely crafted copies of the Bible, two of which—the Codex Vaticanus and the Codex Sinaiticus—survive today.

Constantine's greatest feat after legitimizing the Christian Church was the founding of a new city for this new Christian empire. Although Constantine's march toward total control of the empire began with his triumphant parade into Rome, he did not care for the capital. Born on the frontier and raised in Diocletian's eastern palace, Constantine's visit following the Battle of Milvian Bridge may well have been his first visit to the city. He also took issue with Rome's culture, which was controlled by a powerful ruling class of traditionalists who still did not look kindly on the emperor's new cult. Lastly, Rome was already overcrowded, leaving limited available real estate for the building of his monuments.

Constantine instead looked east for the construction of a new city to inaugurate his empire. The eastern part of the Empire held a number of benefits for Constantine. For one, it was the site of his last political conquest, the defeat of Licinius. Additionally, the East was the birthplace of his favored religion, as well as the section of the empire with the largest congregations of Christians and the site of the most violent and persistent periods of persecution. Constantine decided on a location just northeast of Ilium (Troy) at the entrance to the Black Sea called Byzantion (modern-day Istanbul, Turkey). In the tradition of Romulus and Alexander the Great, Constantine renamed this city in his own honor: Constantinople. This city remained the capital of the Eastern Empire, later called the Byzantine Empire, for a millennium, well after the West had crumbled.

Christianity thrived in Constantinople, where awe-inspiring churches towered over those of other cults. The greatest of

A mosaic of Jesus adorns the Hagia Sophia, one of the great Christian churches in Constantinople. It serves as a mosque in modern-day Istanbul, Turkey.

Constantine and the New Christian Empire    109

these, built by Constantine's son Constantius in 360, was the Hagia Sophia (Church of Holy Wisdom). The Hagia Sophia, damaged by fires and earthquakes, has been rebuilt over the centuries, most notably by Justinian in the sixth century. Its latest iteration is an architectural masterpiece. A complex series of semi-domes join to form a central dome stretching 101 feet (31 meters) across and 160 feet (48.5 meters) tall, and the interior is decorated with colored marble. It was turned into a mosque when the Muslim Turks captured the city in 1453, and was transformed into a museum in 1935.

## Consolidating the Church

Constantine not only rained wealth and gifts on the Christian Church during his reign but also helped shape Christian doctrine. Constantine believed himself to be not only the Christian Church's patron but among its chief religious leaders. According to Eusebius, the emperor often delivered sermons on faith in his palace, apparently to the embarrassment of his non-Christian and Christian courtiers alike. Even more telling, Constantine suggested that one of the churches of Constantinople collect the bodies of Jesus's apostles and bury them in twelve of thirteen coffins, the last of which would be reserved for himself.

Constantine did take several opportunities to take charge and influence the political and philosophical direction of Christianity, which, despite its message of the unity and oneness of God, had itself fractured and splintered over centuries of intermittent persecution. There existed at various times in Christianity's early history a number of sects that, like the late Roman Empire itself, were headed by a variety of leaders vying for control.

One such sect that arose during Constantine's reign was known as Arianism, named after its primary proponent, a priest in Alexandria named Arius. Arius was influenced by Plato's ideals of the divine (see chapter 1) as well as possibly Origen's apologies (see chapter 4). Arius argued that if God the Father is unknowable to imperfect humanity, as Plato argued, then Jesus Christ, who is explained to humanity in the Gospels, cannot also be God. Additionally, if God is one perfect and indivisible whole, then logically he could not have created his Son, Jesus, out of himself. Arius's intellectual argument proved convincing to a number of Christians within the Church of Alexandria, giving the city's bishop, Alexander, reason to worry.

To stem the flow of Christians to Arianism, an **ecumenical** council was convened at Nicaea, southeast of Constantinople, either by Constantine or the bishop of Rome, Pope Sylvester I. Constantine not only wrote to the bishops throughout the empire, asking them to travel to Nicaea with haste to attend the council, but he also presided over the first session and actively participated in the debates there. By the end of the council, the bishops had agreed on an official doctrine of *homoousios*, which argued that God the Father, God the Son (Jesus Christ), and God the Spirit (the Holy Spirit) are all "of one substance." The council also drafted a universal creed of faith, known as the Nicene Creed, to be recited by the faithful, and condemned Arianism as a heresy. As a show of solidarity with the Christian Church, the emperor exiled Arius.

Constantine (*center*) presided over the first ecumenical council at Nicaea.

Another conflict that arose under Constantine was the Donatist Schism in Africa, where persecutions were very harsh. There was division over the status of people who had offered sacrifice to the Roman gods to avoid persecution and others who had appeared to cooperate with the Romans. These people were called "traditors." A group led by Donatus rejected the appointment by the Church in Rome of a bishop for Carthage in 311. The reason was that the bishop in question, Caecilian, had been consecrated by a **traditor**. The Donatist churches broke away from the Roman Church and were then persecuted by Constantine. The persecution, during which there was bloodshed on both sides, lasted only a few years, but the schism lasted for one hundred years. The Donatists were the primary Christian group in Africa during the second half of the fourth century. The schism ended when a council voted to reunite with Rome in 411.

# The Rise of Western Christendom

The threats to the Western Roman Empire that started during the crisis of the third century persisted throughout Christianity's rise to dominance. Barbarian tribes from northern Europe and central Asia continued to press down into Roman-held territories in the Mediterranean basin. During this time, taxes collected from both halves of the empire paid into one treasury, but the emperors in the East got the lion's share while the West's infrastructure and defense went underfunded. In 410, the Germanic tribe known as the Visigoths, under the general Alaric, sacked Rome. The barbarians plundered the city for three days, leaving witnesses around the ancient world speechless. St. Jerome, a Christian priest, historian, and writer who would translate the Greek Bible into Latin, wrote from Palestine, "My tongue sticks to the roof of my mouth." At the moment before the plunge, a hushed silence fell over the West.

The Visigothic Sack was the first of several such invasions of Rome, the center of the Western Empire. The historical question of how and when exactly the Western Roman Empire "fell" is a tricky one. The Eastern Empire survived basically intact for over a millennium in the form of the Byzantine Empire, and even in the West, fragments of the Roman Empire continued in some form or another. (Indeed, the so-called Holy Roman Empire commanded an affiliation of territories in central Europe from the ninth century until the early 1800s.) However, the various barbarian invasions and constant exchanges of power indicate that control of Rome had been so destabilized that it no longer resembled the empire of the past, ushering in a period known as the Middle Ages.

Into this vacuum stepped Christianity, which was by this point the predominant religion in the Roman Empire. Amid the chaos of pillaging barbarians, crumbling empires, and constant warfare, the Christian Church maintained some semblance of civilization for the Western World. In an ironic reversal of fate, Christianity not only survived the empire that had sponsored its persecution but transcended it. Although numerous kingdoms and empires would rise and fall during the Middle Ages, Christianity's power grew considerably. The Catholic Church remained the dominant political power in the West for centuries, and the monarchies that arose from the decline of the Roman Empire clung to it for legitimacy.

# Key Dates in the Persecution of Christians

**753 BCE:** Legendary date of Rome's founding.

**428 BCE:** Jewish state is politically organized in modern-day Israel.

**323 BCE:** Macedonian general Alexander the Great dies; his empire, which includes Greece, Egypt, the Near East (Israel), and parts of Persia and India, is divided among his generals; Greek culture is introduced, beginning the Hellenistic period.

**63 BCE:** The Roman general Pompey conquers Jerusalem; Israel becomes a Roman province.

**31 BCE:** Octavian Augustus defeats his rivals in the civil wars that followed Julius Caesar's assassination, becoming the first emperor of Rome.

**circa 4 BCE**: Estimated year of the birth of Jesus.

**14 CE:** Augustus is deified by the Roman Senate, initiating the long tradition of state-mandated worship of past and present emperors.

**circa 30:** Jesus is executed by Roman prefect of Judaea Pontius Pilate on charges of fomenting political dissent among the Jews; rumors that Jesus was resurrected begin circulating among his followers.

**circa 35:** Saul (Paul) of Tarsus, a Jewish religious scholar, receives a vision of Jesus Christ and converts to Christianity; Paul begins traveling around the Roman Empire, preaching in synagogues and to non-Jews (Gentiles).

**48:** The leaders of Christianity convene the Council of Jerusalem to discuss the matter of Gentiles in the Church, especially the matter of circumcision; they decide, at Paul's urging, conversion does not require circumcision, thus distinguishing Christianity from Judaism.

**50:** The Apostle Paul begins writing letters on faith and correct practice to Christian communities throughout the Roman Empire; these collected letters are the earliest writings of Christianity.

**54:** Nero becomes emperor at the age of sixteen; his initially benevolent reign (directed in large part by his custodians) gradually becomes more brutal as his absolute power feeds his mania.

**58–60:** Paul is taken into custody and transported to Rome to stand trial for charges related to sedition.

**July 19, 64:** A fire breaks out near Rome's Circus Maximus, burning for six days before coming briefly under control, then burning for another three. When the smoke clears, approximately two-thirds of the city lay in ruin. A rumor that Nero started the fire starts to circulate. To counter the rumor, Nero blames the Christians for the fire and initiates a persecution of the religion in Rome.

**circa 65:** The apostles Peter and Paul are likely executed by Nero in or just outside Rome.

**68:** Nero commits suicide, propelling Rome into Civil War.

**circa 70:** The Gospel of Mark, the first account of Jesus's life, is written.

**165:** The apologist St. Justin is martyred in Rome during the persecution under Marcus Aurelius.

**202:** Septimius Severus issues an edict forbidding any more conversions to Judaism or Christianity, kicking off a nine-year persecution.

**203:** St. Perpetua is martyred in Carthage.

**249–251:** Emperor Decius calls for the first empire-wide persecution of Christians.

**257–260:** Valerian's persecution.

**285–286:** Diocletian becomes Emperor and divides the Empire into two administrative halves.

**303:** Diocletian begins the last Roman state-sponsored persecution of Christians, known as the Great Persecution. The violence is concentrated in Diocletian's eastern half of the empire, where Christian communities are largest, and continues in parts of the East for over a decade.

**312:** The Roman general Constantine meets the emperor Maxentius at the Battle of Milvian Bridge outside Rome. Before the battle, Constantine receives a sign from Jesus Christ and orders his soldiers to paint a Christian symbol on their shields. Though outnumbered, they handily defeat Maxentius. Constantine becomes emperor and adopts Christianity as his personal religion.

**313:** Constantine and his eastern counterpart, Licinius, issue the Edict of Milan, guaranteeing equal rights for Christians throughout the empire.

**324:** Constantine defeats Licinius, becoming the sole rule of the Roman Empire; Constantine moves his capital to Byzantium (later known as Constantinople, today known as Istanbul). Constantine begins showering the Christian Church with imperial wealth, and Christianity flourishes.

**325:** The Council of Nicaea convenes to discuss a fringe theology known as Arianism and establish a uniform Christian doctrine. Arianism is condemned as a heresy, and Constantine exiles its proponent, Arius.

**410:** The first sack of Rome by the Germanic Visigoths instigates the Western Roman Empire's gradual collapse. The Christian Church rises during this period of chaos as the only civilizing institution in Europe, becoming the predominant religion and political structure.

**amnesty**  Pardon for people convicted of offenses, especially political.

**apocryphal**  Describing a story whose authenticity is not verified but is nevertheless widely circulated as true.

**apology**  A reasoned argument written to justify one's beliefs or respond to another's accusations.

**apostle**  One of Jesus's twelve original disciples, or another important Christian leader, such as Paul of Tarsus. One sent on a mission.

**Arianism**  An influential early theology based on Platonic philosophy proposed by the Alexandrian priest Arius. It argued that Jesus Christ was neither divine nor of the same substance as God because he was created after God. Arianism was later discredited as a heresy by the Council of Nicaea.

**augury**  The interpretation of omens, such as the flight patterns of birds, especially in ancient pagan religions.

**baptism**  A Christian ritual of initiation in which water and sometimes oil is sprinkled on a person's head or a person is submerged, signifying purification.

**bishop**  A high-ranking member of the Christian Church who oversees a diocese.

**catacomb**  A subterranean cemetery with recesses built into the walls for tombs.

**Christ**  An honorific Greek term meaning "anointed one."

**circumcision**  The ritual removal of a man's foreskin as a rite of entry into a religion, especially Judaism.

**covenant**  An agreement or promise initiated by God with his people.

**crucifixion**  A method of execution widely used by the Romans involving nailing or binding someone to a cross.

**ecumenical**  Involving a number of Christian churches.

**Gentile**  Any person who is not Jewish.

**Gospel**  One of four books in the Christian Bible that document Jesus's life and teachings.

**Hellenistic**  Describing the period from the death of Alexander the Great to the rise of Octavian Augustus, when Greek language and culture flourished from the eastern Mediterranean and Near East to Persia.

**heresy**  Belief or opinion that is contrary to orthodox doctrine.

**martyrdom**  The act of dying for one's faith.

**Messiah**  The prophesied savior of the Jewish religion.

**monotheism**  Belief in one supreme God.

**New Testament**  The second part of the Christian Bible, following the Old Testament, recording the life and teachings of Jesus and his early followers.

**Old Testament**  The Christian term for the Hebrew Bible.

**pagan**  A follower of any religion other than Christianity, Judaism, or Islam; here, a follower of a polytheistic religion.

**passion**  A story relating a saint's suffering and death.

**persecution** Hostility or violence directed at someone or a group of people, especially because of race, politics, or religious beliefs.

**polemic** A verbal or written attack on someone or something, especially the values or beliefs of a certain community.

**polytheism** Belief in a multitude of gods.

**resurrection** To bring a dead person back to life; in Christianity, Jesus bringing himself back to life.

**saint** In Catholic and Orthodox Christianity, a person who is officially recognized after death for his or her virtue and is therefore due honor and veneration.

**scapegoat** A person or group that is blamed for the wrongdoings of others, especially as a matter of expediency.

**sect** A group within a larger religious group with slightly differing beliefs.

**Tanakh** The Hebrew word for the Bible.

**Torah** The law in Judaism as revealed to Moses and documented in the first five books of the Hebrew Bible.

**traditor** A Christian who turned over sacred books and vessels, and fellow Christians to the authorities during the Roman Persecutions.

## Books

Aslan, Reza. *Zealot: The Life and Times of Jesus of Nazareth*. New York: Random House, 2013.

MacCulloch, Diarmaid. *Christianity: The First Three Thousand Years*. New York: Penguin Books, 2010.

Sienkiewicz, Henryk. *Quo Vadis*. Translated by W. S. Kuniczak. New York: Hippocrene Books, 2002.

Wilkens, Robert Louis. *The Christians as the Romans Saw Them*. New Haven, CT: Yale University Press, 2003.

## Websites

### The Christian Catacombs

http://www.vatican.va/roman_curia/pontifical_commissions/archeo/inglese/documents/rc_com_archeo_doc_20011010_cataccrist_en.html
Explore the catacombs from the comfort of a computer. This site, hosted by the Vatican in Rome, discusses the history and architecture of the catacombs and features a number of photographs.

### Internet Ancient History Sourcebook: Christian Origins

http://legacy.fordham.edu/Halsall/ancient/asbook11.asp
This website, hosted by Fordham University, is an exceptional resource for students of early Christianity. Its clickable outline format clearly and succinctly organizes a vast number of links to original Christian and Roman source material by topic.

## Internet Ancient History Sourcebook: Rome

http://legacy.fordham.edu/Halsall/ancient/asbook09.asp
Like its sister site on early Christianity, this site features an outline skewed toward Roman history, from its beginnings to approximately before the rise of Constantine.

# Videos

### History Channel: The Bible

http://www.history.com/shows/the-bible
The History Channel's *The Bible* is a miniseries that dramatizes the life, teachings, and death of Jesus of Nazareth for a popular audience. This site includes the episodes in the series.

### National Geographic Channel: Jesus: Rise to Power

http://channel.nationalgeographic.com/jesus-rise-to-power/
The National Geographic Channel hosts this website on its series about Christianity's rise to prominence. It features several full episodes as well as shorter video clips on a range of topics discussed in this book, including the Great Persecution, the martyrdom of Perpetua, and many more.

### PBS: From Jesus to Christ

http://www.pbs.org/wgbh/pages/frontline/shows/religion
This PBS series explores the historical evidence coming to light about Jesus's life and Christianity's rise to prominence. Each brief episode includes a synopsis, and the website itself offers links to dozens of topics grouped by category.

## SELECTED BIBLIOGRAPHY

## Books

Aslan, Reza. *Zealot: The Life and Times of Jesus of Nazareth.* New York: Random House, 2013.

Brown, Peter. *The Rise of Western Christendom: Triumph and Diversity: A.D. 200–1000.* Malden, MA: Blackwell Publishers, 1996.

Gascoigne, Bamber. *Christianity: A History.* New York: Carroll & Graf Publishers, 2003.

MacCulloch, Diarmaid. *Christianity: The First Three Thousand Years.* New York: Penguin Books, 2010.

Sienkiewicz, Henryk. *Quo Vadis.* Translated by W. S. Kuniczak. New York: Hippocrene Books, 2002.

Wilkens, Robert Louis. *The Christians as the Romans Saw Them.* New Haven, CT: Yale University Press, 2003.

## Online Articles

Biblical Archaeology Society Staff. "Roman Crucifixion Methods Reveal the History of Crucifixion." *Bible History Daily*, July 17, 2011. http://www.biblicalarchaeology.org/daily/biblical-topics/crucifixion/roman-crucifixion-methods-reveal-the-history-of-crucifixion.

Brians, Paul. "Tacitus (c. 55–117 CE): Nero's Persecution of the Christians." Washington State University. Accessed July 14, 2016. http://public.wsu.edu/~brians/world_civ/worldcivreader/world_civ_reader_1/tacitus.html.

Chappell, Bill. "World's Muslim Population Will Surpass Christians This Century, Pew Says." NPR, April 2, 2015. http://www.npr.org/sections/thetwo-way/2015/04/02/397042004/muslim-population-will-surpass-christians-this-century-pew-says.

Cousin, Jean. "Diocletian." *Encylopedia Britannica.* Accessed July 14, 2016. https://www.britannica.com/biography/Diocletian.

"The Death of Alexander the Great." EyeWitness to History. http://www.eyewitnesstohistory.com/alexanderdeath.htm.

The Editors of Encyclopedia Britannica. "Council of Nicaea." *Encyclopedia Britannica.* Accessed July 14, 2016. https://www.britannica.com/event/Council-of-Nicaea-Christianity-325.

———— . "Crucifixion." *Encyclopedia Britannica.* Accessed July 14, 2016. https://www.britannica.com/topic/crucifixion-capital-punishment.

———— . "Nero." *Encyclopedia Britannica.* Accessed July 14, 2016. https://www.britannica.com/biography/Nero-Roman-emperor.

———— . "Spartacus." *Encyclopedia Britannica.* Accessed May 18, 2016. https://www.britannica.com/biography/Spartacus-Roman-gladiator.

"The Fall of Rome: Facts and Fictions." Utah State University. Accessed July 14, 2016. http://www.usu.edu/markdamen/1320hist&civ/chapters/08romfal.htm.

"The Great Fire of Rome: Background." PBS. Accessed July 14, 2016. http://www.pbs.org/wnet/secrets/great-fire-rome-background/1446.

Lebreton, Jules. "St. Justin Martyr." *The Catholic Encyclopedia.* Vol. 8. New York: Robert Appleton Company, 1910. http://www.newadvent.org/cathen/08580c.htm.

"List of Jewish Prophets." Jewish Virtual Library. Accessed May 18, 2016. http://www.jewishvirtuallibrary.org/jsource/Judaism/The_List_of_Prophets.html.

Matthews, J. F. "Constantine I." *Encyclopedia Britannica.* Accessed July 14, 2016. https://www.britannica.com/biography/Constantine-I-Roman-emperor.

McCall, Thomas S. "The Language of the Gospel." Zola Levitt Ministries, May 1997. https://www.levitt.com/essays/language

Moore, Edward. "Origen of Alexandria (185–254 C.E.)." Internet Encyclopedia of Philosophy. Accessed July 14, 2016. http://www.iep.utm.edu/origen-of-alexandria.

Pelikan, Jaroslav Jan. "Jesus." *Encyclopedia Britannica*. Accessed July 14, 2016. https://www.britannica.com/biography/Jesus.

Prat, Ferdinand. "Origen and Origenism." *The Catholic Encyclopedia*. Vol. 11. New York: Robert Appleton Company, 1911. http://www.newadvent.org/cathen/11306b.htm.

Schlabach, Gerald W. "Celsus' View of Christians and Christianity." Bluffton University, August 8, 1997. http://www.bluffton.edu/~humanities/1/celsus.htm

Shrewing, W. H. "Medieval Sourcebook: St. Perpetua: *The Passions of Saints Perpetua and Felicity*." Fordham University. Accessed July 14, 2016. http://legacy.fordham.edu/halsall/source/perpetua.asp.

"St. Maximillian." Catholic Online.org. Accessed July 14, 2016. http://www.catholic.org/saints/saint.php?saint_id=5018.

Telushkin, Joseph. "Jewish Concepts: The Messiah." Jewish Virtual Library. http://www.jewishvirtuallibrary.org/jsource/Judaism/messiah.html.

Wasson, Donald L. "Constantine I." Ancient History Encyclopedia, April 19, 2013. http://www.ancient.eu/Constantine_I.

——— . "Diocletian." Ancient History Encyclopedia, February 2, 2014. http://www.ancient.eu/Diocletian.

Woods, David. "St. Maximilian of Tebessa." University College Cork. Accessed July 14, 2016. http://www.ucc.ie/archive/milmart/Maximilian.html.

# INDEX

place in the Holy Trinity, 95, 111

as political radical, 27–31

resurrection, 31–33, 35

and sacrifice, 51

and symbols, 53, 55

John the Baptist, 27, 28

Judaea, 5, 6, 10, 11, 12, 47, 56, 59, 79

Judaism, overview of, 11–18

Justin Martyr, St., 90–92, **91**, 95, 97

Lawrence, St., **88**

martyrdom, origins of, 68–69

Maximian, 84, 86, 87, 102, 103

Maximilian of Theveste, St., 96–97

**Messiah**, 6, 17, 18, 37

**monotheism**, 12 , **93**, **98**

Moses, 13, 14, 15, 47

Nero, 60–63, **63**, 64, 66, 67, 68, 74, 78, 80, 82

**New Testament** (Christian Bible), 26, 38

**Old Testament** (Hebrew Bible), 12, 16, 18

orgies, 50, 52

Origen of Alexandria, 92–95, **93**, 97, 111

**pagan**, 55, 56, 73, 87, 90, 93, 94, 95, 97, 98

**passion**, 69

Paul of Tarsus, St., 36–37, **37**, 38–39, 46, 57, 66, 73, 93

Perpetua, St., 69–72, **70**, 83

**persecution**, periods of, 80–81, 82–83, 84–85, 87, 102, 106

Peter, Saint, 27, 33, 39, **58**, 66

Phoenicians, 19–20

Pilate, Pontius, 6, 30, 47, 59

Plato, 20–23, 24, 89, 91, 93, 97, **99**, 111

Pliny the Younger, 73–75, 82

**polemic**, 90

**polytheism**, 12

*religio licita*, 57

**resurrection**, 31–33, 35, 101

Rome, founding myth of, 40–45, 47

Sabines, 42–43, **43**, 44

Sator Square, 53–54, 55

**scapegoat**, 63

**sect**, 16, 36, 39, 52, 82, 110, 111

"Sermon on the Mount," 27–28

syllabic writing, 19–20

symbols, early Christian, 52–55

**Tanakh**, 12, 16

**Torah**, 12, 13, 17, 18, 36

**traditor**, 112

Trajan, 74, 75, 82

**Andrew Coddington** studied English, writing, and classics at Canisius College. He has written a number of books for Cavendish Square on a variety of topics, including history and ancient cultures and religions. He lives in Buffalo, New York, with his wife and dog.